PRAISE FOR DIGITAL OPERATIONS

"Michael has created something CEOs actually need - a practical roadmap that shows you exactly how to prepare your operations for AI without the tech jargon. The case studies are the best part of the book, showing real companies getting real results. This isn't another theoretical framework; it's a step-by-step guide that takes you from operational chaos to digital foundation and beyond. For any CEO trying to figure out their AI strategy, this gives you the clarity to know where you are and what needs to happen next."

—David Hilbish, *5x CEO & Fractional Executive Presume Nothing Advisors*

"This book nails the sweet spot between tactics and strategy. The 5 Levels framework finally explains why so many automation projects fail, they're trying to automate chaos instead of first building a foundation. If you're tired of bouncing between sales and fulfillment, drowning in operational debt, this book shows you exactly how to systematically climb out. It's the strategic companion to tactical automation that I wish I'd had years ago. Every overwhelmed entrepreneur needs this roadmap."

—Uzair Ahmed, *Founder of instaMek Mobile Mechanics and Cottonwood Automation*

i

"This book is loaded with practical value. Michael nailed it—I'd recommend it 10 out of 10. He gives you the framework to get moving with automation and AI, but more importantly, he shows why building the foundation first is non-negotiable. This isn't theory. It's the real-world roadmap to skip the chaos that trips up most growing companies."

—Malcolm Peace, *Small Business Enthusiast and President of Tsetserra Growth Partners*

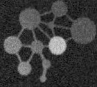

Digital Operations Playbook

AI Readiness for SMBs

Michael Greenberg　　　Brandon White

Paperback ISBN:

E-book ISBN:

1st edition, October 2025

DEDICATION

For those we have loved and lost

TABLE OF CONTENTS

ABOUT THE AUTHORS

Michael Greenberg is a serial entrepreneur and founder of 3rdBrain.co with over a decade experience and a proven track record of success across industries. Michael founded 3rd Brain Digital Operations in 2022 after building out operational playbooks at Podcast360 and GrowthAssistant. He spearheads the frameworks, tools, and educational development for integrating AI into business workflows at 3rd Brain.

Brandon White is an accomplished serial entrepreneur and tech industry veteran with a career spanning nearly three decades. He founded Worldwide Angler in 1996, pioneering social networking for anglers, and has since achieved two successful exits. His diverse background includes venture capital, angel investing, and marketing leadership at AOL. He is CEO at 3rd Brain Digital Operations, 3rdbrain.co

BUILDING AN
AI-READY DIGITAL OPERATION

We've entered a world where **AI and automation** is reshaping entire business models. Without a solid data layer foundation, **plugging AI into a messy digital foundation** amplifies chaos leading to failed projects, poor adoption, flawed outputs, ballooning costs, and disillusioned teams.

Over the past three years I have helped dozens of companies build stable foundations for automation and AI to accelerate their businesses. From 30-person manufacturing firms growing top line with Level 4 automated workflows to 100-employee marketing agencies finally escaping spreadsheet hell.

Inside this book you will find the frameworks, tools, strategies, and best practices we have developed to lead a thoughtful, human-first transformation for AI readiness.

By the end of the book you will have a clear roadmap and toolbox designed for owners and managers of small/mid-sized businesses to **upgrade your digital operations** so that when AI is implemented, it soars vs. sputters.

Shared Ground: Where Are You Today?

Whether you're the one driving the strategy, designing the workflows, or implementing the systems, you'll find actionable guidance here. If you're working together across functions, this shared language will help your team align on where you're going, and how you'll get there. No matter your role, you need a baseline and shared understanding of one thing:

Where is your organization is today, and what does it need to get to the next level?

Digital transformation happens in stages. If you skip those stages by bolting on automation/AI before you've built the right foundation, you will not get efficiency, you will get chaos.

We call that hidden cost of premature or rushed implementation **operational debt.**

Path 1: The Owner-Operator

You own the business. You run the business. Now, you're ready to improve the business.

Maybe you started it, inherited it, or acquired it. And you're the one responsible for making it better.

For you, this book is both a strategic map and guide. Start with the Executive Summary and Visual Map to understand the big picture. Then, go through the book sequentially. It helps you lead your team through the transformation with confidence and avoid common pitfalls.

Start with: Executive Overview → Main Book → Workbook as Needed

Path 2: The Strategic Executive (Director, VP, GM)

You lead a department or function inside a growing company. You're not hands-on with implementation, but you need to know how digital transformation will affect your team, your priorities, and your resources.

This book gives you the frameworks to think strategically, support initiatives in your area, and communicate clearly with your implementers and leadership. You can skip the how-to tutorials and focus on planning.

Start with: Executive Overview → Main Book

Path 3: The Implementer (Ops, IT, PMs, Chiefs of Staff)

You're the one who will turn this strategy into working systems. You're technical enough to understand tradeoffs but you need your team and leadership to understand them too.

This book gives you the language to explain operational debt, make the case for investments, and prioritize work. You'll want to read the entire book and use the Workbook to guide execution, track progress, and level up specific departments.

Start with: Executive Overview → Main Book → Workbook

The Flywheel: What Happens at Level 3 and Beyond

Most organizations spend years stuck in Level 1 or 2 running on spreadsheets, legacy tools, and disconnected workflows. These companies work hard, but progress is slow and chaotic.

Everything changes at **Level 3**. It's the tipping point where core workflows are unified, your systems talk to each other, and your team operates from a single source of truth.

Once you reach this point, a self-reinforcing cycle begins. We call it the **Digital Operations Flywheel**, as displayed in the flowchart on the next page.

```
┌─────────────┐      ┌──────────────────┐   ┌──────────────────┐
│   Choose    │      │  "Where Are We??"│   │ "How do we Level │
│   Digital   │ ───▶ │ Assess Department│─▶ │      Up?"        │
│ Operations  │      │ Role, or Company │   │ Align with 3 Cs, │
└─────────────┘      │ using 5 Levels.  │   │ Develop 5 Pillars│
       │             └──────────────────┘   └──────────────────┘
       ▼
┌─────────────┐       PEOPLE -> PROCESS -> TOOLS
│   REACH     │       BUILD LEVEL 3 FOUNDATION
│   LEVEL 3   │
│             │       1. Talent Strategy
└─────────────┘       2. Workflow Optimization
       │              3. Digital Architecture
       ▼
┌──────────────┐   ┌──────────────────┐   ┌──────────────────┐
│ Consistency: │   │    Clarity:      │   │    Capacity:     │
│• Documentation│─▶│• Clean Data      │─▶│• Less Stress     │
│• Data Standards│  │• Accurate        │   │• More Work Done  │
│              │   │  Dashboards      │   │                  │
└──────────────┘   └──────────────────┘   └──────────────────┘
       │                                            │
       ▼              DIGITAL OPERATIONS
┌─────────────┐       FLYWHEEL ACCELERATION
│   REACH     │
│  LEVEL 4+   │       1. Talent Strategy
│             │       2. Knowledge Management
└─────────────┘       3. AI Automation
       │
       ▼
┌──────────────┐   ┌──────────────────┐   ┌──────────────────┐
│  Automated   │   │Intelligent       │   │Unlimited Capacity:│
│ Consistency: │   │Clarity:          │   │                  │
│• 24/7        │─▶ │• Automated       │─▶│• Automation of   │
│ Workflows for│   │ Reporting with AI│   │ core operational │
│ automatable  │   │ Analysis         │   │ workflows        │
│ processes    │   │                  │   │                  │
└──────────────┘   └──────────────────┘   └──────────────────┘
```

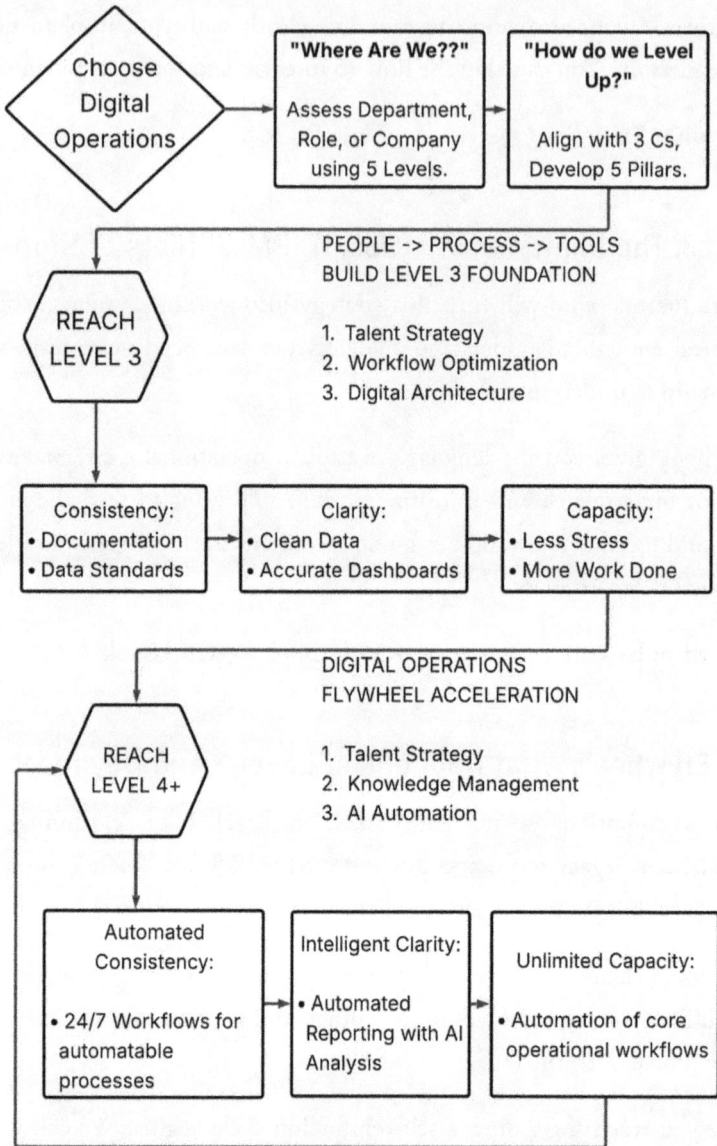

- At **Level 3**, you establish **Consistency** through standardized workflows and integrated systems.

- That consistency unlocks **Clarity** real-time visibility, better decisions, and more trust in your data.

- And with clarity, you gain **Capacity** you automate, delegate, and expand.

Each cycle of this flywheel gives you more leverage to improve your business.

At **Levels 4 and 5**, automation and AI supercharge each phase of the loop.

Your first mission is simple:

Get to Level 3. That's when everything starts to click.

The Road Ahead

The Executive Overview reviews all the core frameworks at the 30,000ft level in the next section.

Chapter 1 sets the stage with the **5 Levels**, illustrating why you can't skip straight to advanced AI if you're stuck in Level 1–2 chaos.

Chapter 2 explores **Consistency, Clarity, and Capacity**; the key benchmarks to track as you evolve.

Chapter 3 breaks down the **Foundational Pillars** (Talent Strategy, Workflow Optimization, Digital Architecture) and shows how they get you to **Level 3**.

Chapter 4 continues on with the Advanced Pillars (Knowledge Management, AI Automation) to reach **Level 4 and 5**.

Chapter 5 puts it all together into a process of planning quarterly level ups.

The Appendices expand on the client case studies with complete transformations as well as useful tools, guides, and workbooks with **hands-on exercises**.

EXECUTIVE OVERVIEW

This book provides a series of strategic frameworks for owners and managers of small/mid-sized businesses to **upgrade their digital operations** so that they can continue to grow as AI improves and integrates with our lives.

Where You Are: The 5 Levels of Digital Operations

Through years of consulting with manufacturers, agencies, and service companies, we've observed organizations progress through 5 levels of digital operations maturity:

Level	Name	Characteristics
1	Information Silos	Disconnected software or paper-based workflows; high error rates and zero real-time visibility
2	Connectable Cloud	Basic cloud solutions in place but not fully connected; scattered documentation and partial adoption
3	Unified Data	Integrated systems with a single source of truth; consistent workflows, significant error reduction

Level	Name	Characteristics
4	Automated Workflows	Deep automation for routine tasks; humans step in mainly for exceptions; capacity expands significantly
5	AI-Powered Operations	Advanced AI handles complex decision-making; minimal manual oversight for day-to-day processes

It's tempting to jump straight to Level 5, **but skipping steps leads to "garbage in, garbage out" and rampant operational debt throughout.**

Why You're Investing: Consistency → Clarity → Capacity

As you level up your **People→Process→Tools**, the 3Cs represent the results:

Consistency: Fewer errors, standardized data formats, uniform workflows.

Clarity: Real-time visibility, unified dashboards, trust in data.

Capacity: Freed from repetitive tasks, teams can handle more work.

At Level 4 and 5, AI and automation often brings a 5-10x+ capacity gain in key workflows.

What and How to Improve: The 5 Pillars Framework

We organize digital operations capabilities into **five pillars,** each with 3 key subcomponents covered later in the book.

1. Talent Strategy
2. Workflow Optimization
3. Digital Architecture
4. Knowledge Management
5. AI Automation

Early on (Levels 1–3), **Pillars 1–3** take center stage to eliminate silos, unify data, and standardize procedures.

People → Process → Tools: Getting to Level 3

1. **People: Talent Strategy:** Define roles, upskill staff, secure leadership buy-in
   "Don't buy fancy software if your team can't or won't use it."

2. **Process: Workflow Optimization:** Document, standardize, refine
   "A well-documented process is your insurance against confusion."

3. **Tools: Digital Architecture:** Only after your people understand the workflow do you integrate or automate
   "We use technology to accelerate clarity, not to fix confusion."

A similar methodology can be applied to go from Level 3 to Level 4/5, with high skill talent focused on Knowledge Management and AI Automation instead.

Real-World Snapshots

Throughout this book, we'll illustrate key lessons from six clients on their journey from Level 1 to (in one case) Level 5. Each is expanded in the Appendices after Chapter 5:

Western Siding

Industry: Manufacturing & Contracting (Siding)
Size: $5+ million revenue
Starting Point: Level 1
Achievement: Reached Level 4 in sales; expanded via global outreach team
Results: Errors eliminated, stronger communication across departments, out-of-state expansion

Fitness Marketing Advisors

Industry: Business Services (Fitness niche)
Size: 20+ employees
Starting Point: Level 1
Achievement: Digital Architecture & Workflow Optimization
Results: 40+ hours/week saved, streamlined client onboarding, Level 3 data unification

Quick Serve Franchise

Industry: Restaurant Holding Company
Size: 50+ locations
Starting Point: Level 1
Achievement: Level 4 in accounting/finance processes, Level 3 throughout
Results: 90% reduction in manual work, 60+ hours/week saved

Marketing Agency Rollup

Industry: Digital Marketing
Size: 100+ employees
Starting Point: Level 2
Achievement: Achieved Level 4 in core delivery workflows
Results: 50% error reduction, doubled client capacity without increasing headcount

Digital PR Startup

Industry: Public Relations
Size: 5-person "born digital" team
Starting Point: Level 3, designed for integrated AI-driven workflows
Achievement: Reached Level 5 with ghostwriting agents & automated outreach
Results: 40% smaller pods handling 10x the client load, minimal overhead

Podcast Production Agency

Industry: Media Production
Size: 10 employees
Starting Point: Level 2, manual assignment & tracking
Achievement: Level 4 with AI-assisted audio editing workflows
Results: 95% fewer missed deadlines, 40% overall productivity boost

CHAPTER 1

WHY DIGITAL
OPERATIONS MATTERS *RIGHT NOW*

We're on the cusp of an advanced AI takeoff. Systems that once seemed futuristic will hit the market this year and throughout the decade ahead.

If you're currently a small or mid-sized business (SMB) owner or manager, you've probably felt the pinch of those inefficiencies endlessly copying data between spreadsheets, waiting on updates from Bob (who has that one crucial file), or chasing down a missing invoice at 6 p.m. on a Tuesday.

In other words:

1. **Digital chaos** → wasted time, lost revenue, confused data, stressed teams, copy/paste hell

2. **A robust digital operation** → a near-future advantage where you can plug AI into a stable foundation to plug in AI

This first chapter is your orientation. We'll explore why Digital Operations, how to know where you are using the 5 Levels, and what real-world transformations look like when you prepare for this new era of AI.

Western Siding: Operations, Not Transformation

Who They Are: A 2nd generation family owned 38-person, 34 year old siding company. They're known for quality craftsmanship in the region but not necessarily speed or digital savvy.

Core Pain: Each department picked software with little oversight or integration. The resulting patchwork is riddled with manual processes.

Daily Nightmare:

- Production logs in one system, finance in another, HR in yet another and no shared data pipelines.

- Purchase orders get handwritten and then typed into an ancient ERP only a few employees know how to operate.

- Shipping errors regularly occur because inventory and purchase updates rarely sync across the entire organization.

The floor manager noted: "We have all this fancy software, but nobody trusts the data to be up-to-date. I get calls from accounts about an order update daily."

> **The Problem:** Whether it's a brand-savvy startup or a tried-and-true manufacturer, siloed **data and disjointed processes** stops them from scaling up.

Last year, they hired us to take their team to Level 3 after they lost over $60,000 to unsigned change orders. We built them a CRM, integrated with a signing tool, and their ERP for manufacturing. Every change order and contract has been signed since.

What is Digital Operations?

Digital Operations is the discipline of designing, implementing, educating, and aligning an organization around a cohesive digital ecosystem.

- **Automation**: Minimizing grunt work, no more copy/paste marathons or endless data entry.

- **AI Tools & Models**: Leveraging advanced tools to handle forecasts, scheduling, or nuanced decision-making.

- **Remote/Global Talent**: Finding specialized skill sets worldwide and on the web, not just in your zip code.

- **Streamlined Processes**: Documenting how work flows so everyone follows consistent best practices.

Think of your business as a house.

Digital Operations is the foundation, wiring, and plumbing. You might not show it off to dinner guests, but if it's faulty or outdated, you'll soon have serious problems. It's the invisible architecture that connects the people, processes, tools, and data behind your business.

The 5-Levels of Digital Operations

Level 1-2 Organizations typically suffer from unaligned growth, tribal knowledge, and technology decisions over time:

- Tools were chosen before processes were understood
- Processes exist only in people's heads
- People lack skills to use systems effectively

This creates **"Operational Debt"** from quick fixes and workarounds. The interest on this debt is measured in wasted time, duplicated effort, and missed opportunities. Eventually it will need to be paid, normally in the form of a slower level up.

Level 3 represents the successful completion of unified digital operations infrastructure:

- Your People have clear roles and adequate digital skills
- Your Processes are documented and standardized
- Your Tools are integrated with clean, consistent data

Once you've reached Level 3 you can begin investing in advanced AI capabilities or complex automation without worry.

Just like a house starts with a foundation and eventually becomes a complete building, organizations evolve through distinct "levels" of digital operations maturity based around **Documentation, Data Management, and Software.**

"Leveling up" a role, department, or company has clear benefits:

1. **Future-Proof Foundation**: You can't harness advanced AI or high-level automations if your underlying data is not consistent.

2. **Fewer Errors & Faster Decisions**: Clear data across tools means real-time visibility. Everyone trusts the same dashboard.

3. **Better ROI**: Less time wasted on double-entry or repetitive tasks, more time on strategic initiatives. Automation and integration improve capacity.

Getting to level 3 will take 6-18 months for most organizations under 100 employees. Few are even at level 2 companywide when we start.

The 5 Levels helps set us for success by showing us where we are and giving us a common vision of where operations are going. The 3 Cs (Chapter 2) will give us a clear measure of what the results will look like. The 5 Pillars

(Chapter 3 and 4) give us a capabilities checklist to help navigate the transition level by level.

Many want to accelerate key departments to level 4 rather than going for a unified data layer companywide first, but that sort of unbalanced transformation can cause issues even if egos are well managed.

Level 1. Information Silos

Independent Operations

Software: Digital, analog, or paper tools that cannot be 100% integrated.

Workflow Documentation: Processes often exist only in employees' heads; may have some checklists written down

Data Management: No data management processes. Scattered databases.

How Companies Find Themselves Here

Let everyone choose software without considering the entire company, just what they like. Scale quickly with key employees holding onto processes in their heads instead of documenting them. Avoid change because "this is how we've always done it."

Typical Impact

- **High error rates:** 10 different versions of the same customer data.
- **Staff frustration:** nobody knows where to find key info.
- **Reactionary firefighting:** always feeling one glitch away from chaos.
- **Lots of Copy/Paste:** Data duplication is part of the process
- **Outdated SOPs:** documentation is never up to date

Analogy: It's like having five "junk drawers" in your kitchen. Everything's there, but everything's still a mess.

People→Process→Tools Misalignment: At Level 1, organizations typically jump straight to tools without defining who should use them (People) or how they should be used (Process). The result? Software sits unused or misused, creating even more operational debt.

Level 2. Connectable Cloud

Software: Cloud-based tools capable of integration but not yet fully connected.

Workflow Documentation: Basic documentation starts to emerge; some high-level processes mapped.

Data Management: CRM, ERP, accounting and other storage chosen. Data not cleaned.

> **Note:** Many "remote first" but are often stuck at this level, juggling multiple apps that don't communicate optimally. CRM, Work Management, and other basic tools offer all-in-one solutions to leapfrog whole departments to level 3 but require well documented processes so everyone knows where to put things.

How To Get Here

Choose the right software. Make sure everything can integrate and has full data access via API (Application Programming Interface, how web tools talk to each other) or automation platform access.

Typical Impact

Level 2 is a starting point for most and a quick stop for those on the way to Level 3, so getting familiar with the new tools is the top priority.

People→Process→Tools Progress: At Level 2, organizations begin addressing the People and Process elements, but often unevenly. They might train staff on individual tools but haven't yet created comprehensive workflows that connect those tools together.

Level 3. Unified Data Layer

What truly makes Level 3 transformative is the unified foundation it creates:

Software: Integrated cloud-based tools with single points of truth for data.

Workflow Documentation: Systems map documentation for workflows and data; clear organizational structure.

Data Management: Customer and key ops data is auto cleaned on input or transfer. Single points of truth chosen.

Level 3 In Plain English: Everyone sees the same scoreboard, so decision-making is faster, more accurate, and less political ("Wait, whose numbers are right?").

How to Get Here

Document the customer and data journeys behind all core business processes. Then integrate and automate the data transfer between them.

For most department sizes (~30) or smaller teams, going from Level 2 to Level 3 will take approximately 9 months. The majority of this time is in education and adoption, so digital native departments who adapt quickly may be able to get there in just a few months.

Typical Impact

- Eliminate Copy/Paste Hell, Automate Data Clarity
- Real-time visibility: the team can trust company dashboards
- Reduced duplication: saving thousands of staff hours a year
- Clarifies team workflows and clean data improve consistency
- 50%+ work can be done remotely. 20%+ can be automated.

People → Process → Tools Alignment: Level 3 represents the successful completion of the first People → Process → Tools cycle. Your team understands their roles, follows documented processes, and uses integrated tools that support those processes. This creates the consistency, clarity, and initial capacity gains we'll explore in Chapter 2.

Level 4: Automated Workflows

Software: Automated tools handle many processes, but are operated by a human.

Workflow Documentation: Detailed process maps and workflow documentation are in place.

Data Management: Customer and operational data cleaned regularly. 100% vital data clarity.

> **Quick Example**: A client signs a contract, and a chain reaction is triggered -> project tasks are created, invoices scheduled, Slack channels opened. All without a single manual input.

How to Get Here

Checklists and flowcharts rule level 4 evolutions. Expanding on your documentation **from SOPs for humans to those detailed enough for machines.**

The big leap from Level 3 to 4 is all in the process documentation. Now you have to go beyond data flows to document step by step processes with decision trees for automation. This is an iterative process for most workflows, with the number of edge cases requiring human help dropping with each successive version.

Typical Impact

- Most work that can be remote has been moved to a global team and/or workflows have been automated.

- 20–30% of your to-do list simply disappears, handled by rules-based or AI-driven automation.

- Staff morale climbs; nobody enjoys repetitive data tasks or constant system toggling.

- More "brain space" for strategic or creative work causes team capacity to rise.

People → **Process** → **Tools**: Level 4 requires more development and customization, process documentation, including decision trees, and more advanced tools capable of automation.

It can also unlock 10-20x capacity increases for key workflows.

Level 5. AI Automation

Software: AI-integrated tools using business specific models. As automated as safely possible. Minimal human oversight.

Workflow Documentation: Comprehensive documentation including edge cases and exceptions for AI training.

Data Management: Data management is fully automated for all possible processes

> **Caution:** AI thrives on **clean data**. If you have a messy foundation, many tools will produce messy (or even outright false) results. That's why early levels matter so much.

How to Get Here

Once you are at level 3 or 4 you can begin to see the vision for level 5 in that particular role or process. It will often take the form of internal tools that mimic coworkers via workflow specific interface.

Level 5 may require fine tuning or other advanced AI manipulation. These require clean high quality data sets that can take months to build out.

Typical Impact

- Automate the majority of remote capable processes.
- Scale exponentially while rarely requiring new hires.
- Improved cashflow and profit margins, averaging ~5% for SMBs under 250 employees.

People → Process → Tools Mastery: Level 5 represents the full realization of both People → Process → Tools cycles. You have specialized AI talent, comprehensive processes including edge cases and exceptions, and advanced AI tools that can operate with minimal human oversight.

Western Siding: Scaling Sales & Building a Global Team

Remember the 34-year-old siding company that was struggling with siloed processes and duplicate data entries? After months of documentation, data cleanup, and workflow integrations, they're firmly at **Level 3**.

Single Source of Truth: All purchase orders, inventory updates, and customer data now sync between a central CRM and ERP. No more guesswork on who has the right version of a contract.

Real-Time Dashboards: The leadership team can see daily or weekly revenue forecasts, job progress, and shipping updates at a glance.

Remote-Friendly Processes: With everything standardized and documented, they brought on a global support team to handle routine tasks like following up on small orders or checking inventory counts.

Moving Sales to Level 4

Now that operations are stable, they're accelerating sales processes to **Level 4**. Their new outbound strategy includes tapping into **near shore (LATAM) global talent** to distribute and introduce their products to new channel partners. Automated workflows trigger once a lead is qualified. Emails, sample shipment requests, and even initial invoices are generated without staff intervention.

> *"Before, we couldn't handle more than a few leads a day without drowning in paperwork. Now the system routes everything."* Owner + CEO

Their progression from Level 3 to Level 4 in sales was only possible because they first established a solid foundation. They followed the natural People

$\rightarrow$ Process $\rightarrow$ Tools sequence rather than trying to automate broken or undocumented processes.

Digital PR Startup: Born at Level 4

Imagine launching a company already equipped with integrated tools and AI-based workflows, that's the reality for a new Digital PR startup. From day one, they built a **Level 4** foundation:

1. **Automated Media Outreach**: Their AI-driven platform combs through media databases to find the right journalists and outlets, personalizing each pitch.

2. **Internal Pods, 10x Capacity**: Each specialized "pod" can service 10-20x the clients they handled a year ago because they rely on AI to handle the repetitive tasks like copywriting press releases or segmenting target audiences.

3. **End-to-End Visibility**: Account managers see campaign performance in real time, allowing them to pivot quickly.

Their ongoing challenge is ensuring that as automation grows, the human elements of relationship-building and creative strategy remain front-and-center.

Key Insight: Even this "born digital" company had to make deliberate choices about roles, workflows, and tools before implementing advanced AI. They didn't skip the People$\rightarrow$Process$\rightarrow$Tools methodology; they just applied it from the outset.

Data Matters More Than Ever

It's not just about "saving time" or "being more efficient" (though both are worthy goals). The **rapid evolution of AI**, where advanced generative models or near-AGI might be commercialized, means companies with shaky digital foundations risk falling behind.

Level 3+ guarantees that foundation.

- **AI's Appetite for Clean Data**: Tools like ChatGPT, Claude, and domain-specific AI thrive on accurate, consistent data. If your data is messy, AI outcomes will be messy (or downright unusable).

- **Scalability & Competitiveness**: Companies at Level 3 or 4 can quickly integrate new AI features, outpacing rivals stuck in manual processes.

- **Future-Proofing**: Even if you're not an "AI-first" organization today, you'll want to be ready to plug in new capabilities. A cohesive digital backbone ensures you can seize opportunities without constant rework.

As of mid-2025 when I am writing this, it seems likely that we are at the inflection point in AI development. Embodied AI with humanoid robots, goal oriented agents, and drop in AI workers are all on the 5 year time horizon with alpha versions for most already available.

> **Hard Takeoff Mindset**: Think of it as building the runway before the supersonic jets arrive. If your runway is in disrepair, you can't land or launch anything big even if the technology is at your doorstep.

Exercise: Where Are *You* Right Now?
Digital Operations Self-Assessment Checklist

Check all statements that currently apply to your organization. Each checked item equals one point.

1. People & Team Structure

☐   There is a documented plan for digital skills training

☐   Team members are comfortable adopting new technology

☐   There are designated owners for digital processes

☐   You have access to technical talent when needed

☐   Digital operations has executive support

☐   An internal draftsman, architect, or equivalent role exists internally

2. Process Documentation

☐   Core business processes are documented in writing, flowcharts, and/or checklists

☐   Process documentation is stored in a central location

☐   Documentation includes step-by-step instructions

☐   Process exceptions and edge cases are documented

☐   Documentation is regularly reviewed and updated

☐   New team members can follow processes without extensive training

3. Technology Systems

☐   Core business software is cloud-based

☐   Different departments can easily share data

☐   Software licenses and access are properly managed

☐   Systems can be accessed securely from anywhere

☐   Key software tools can connect to each other

☐   There is a documented technology stack

4. Data Management

☐   Data entry is automated where possible

☐   Data is validated automatically

☐   Reports can be generated automatically

☐   Data flows automatically between systems

☐   Data is consistently formatted across systems

☐   There is a single source of truth for key data

5. Automation Implementation

☐   Repetitive tasks are automated

☐   Workflows trigger automatically based on events

☐   Team members spend minimal time on data entry

☐   Errors from manual processes are rare

☐   Complex processes are partially automated

☐   Resources are focused on high-value work

Scoring & Next Steps

Total Score: _____/30

Next Steps Based on Score:

- 0-10: Focus on documenting processes and choosing good software
- 11-20: Implement integrate core systems and maintain data clarity
- 21-30: Explore advanced automation and optimization opportunities

This assessment is meant to give you a general sense of your digital operations maturity. Use it as a starting point for discussions about improvement opportunities, not an absolute diagnostic device.

Recap: Digital Operations 101

Digital Operations is the discipline of architecting and implementing a cohesive digital ecosystem that connects the people, processes, tools, and data behind your business.

Level	Software	Documentation	Data Management
1 - Information Silos	Digital or analog tools that cannot be 100% integrated.	Processes often exist only in employees' heads; may have some checklists written down	No data management processes. Scattered databases.

Level	Software	Documentation	Data Management
2 -Connectable Cloud	Cloud-based tools capable of integration, but not yet fully connected.	Basic documentation starts to emerge; high-level processes mapped	CRM, ERP, accounting and other storage chosen. Data not cleaned.
3 – Unified Data Layer	Integrated cloud-based tools with single points of truth for data.	Systems map documentation for workflows and data; clear organizational structure.	Customer and key ops data is auto cleaned on input or transfer. Single points of truth chosen.
4 - Automated Workflow	Integrated tools with automated processes, human oversight.	Detailed process maps and workflow documentation.	Customer and operational data is cleaned regularly. 100% vital data clarity.
5 - AI Operations	AI-integrated tools using business specific models. As automated as safely possible.	Comprehensive documentation including edge cases and exceptions for AI training.	Data management is fully automated for all possible processes.

Digital Operations may never grace the cover of flashy magazines, but once you see the transformation in time saved and morale improved you'll never look back.

Become obsessed with automation, more advanced AI, and more ways for your people to do their best work.

The Self-Assessment Checklist will help identify immediate next steps you can take. I recommend picking one "red flag" item to fix this month.

Even small steps can generate massive momentum.

Next Up: The 3 Cs of Digital Operations

Now that you know where you stand within the 5 Levels, it's time to chart the path to your next level.

In chapter 2, we'll dive into The "3 Cs" (Consistency, Clarity, Capacity) that encompass the core results of Digital Operations.

If you're feeling overwhelmed: That's okay! This is a journey that many SMBs begin at a slower pace. The important part is recognizing your current operational level and deciding to address it methodically.

Remember: The next five years will reshape entire industries with AI advancements.

Get your operations to Level 3, the flywheel will follow from there.

In Chapters 3 and 4 we'll explore the 5 Pillars, a capabilities framework showing you exactly what is needed to implement at each level.

CHAPTER 2

THE 3 CS
(CONSISTENCY → CLARITY → CAPACITY)

The 3 Cs (**Consistency, Clarity**, and **Capacity**) are north stars of stability in your business, that pave the way for sustainable growth.

We'll start with a reality-check, look at "before" scenarios of struggling organizations, dig deep into the 3 Cs, then revisit their transformations. Finally, we'll connect this all to the journey you started in Chapter 1 to set your team in motion.

The Chaos of Disconnected Operations

"What should have been simple tasks became hours-long projects just to gather information from different systems. Our people were spending more time managing tools than helping clients."

This was the reality for **Fitness Marketing Advisors**, a consulting/coaching business advising gym owners and trainers on business operations. They started as a one-person company and bootstrapped themselves to 20+ employees, but found themselves trapped in **Operational Debt**:

- **Tool Fragmentation:** Different teams were using different systems. Marketing used Coschedule, customer service used Helpdesk, training materials lived in Trainual, and communication happened in Slack with no central connection point.

- **Duplicate Work:** The disconnected nature of their tools meant people were entering the same information multiple times across platforms. "Wait, did you update that in Keap or just in Slack?" became a common question.

- **Cross-Department Friction:** Without a unified system, divisions of the company struggled to collaborate efficiently. Marketing couldn't easily see what Sales had promised clients, and Operations had no visibility into upcoming content needs.

- **Scalability Roadblock:** As they grew from a solopreneur to a 20+ person operation, their early-stage tools were buckling under the pressure. What worked for 5 people was actively hindering them at 20.

This is a textbook example of Level 1-2 digital operations: scattered data, inconsistent processes, and teams that don't trust what other departments tell them. The result? A business where growth becomes painful rather than exciting.

3Cs Show Results

Even with all the chaos, there is a way out. Once you integrate and organize your data at Level 3 (Unified Data Layer) things get much easier.

Think of the 3 Cs as a chain reaction. Without **Consistency**, you can't have real **Clarity**; if your data is messy, your dashboards are misleading. Without **Clarity**, you can't confidently identify bottlenecks and unlock **Capacity**. You'd be scaling blind.

- **Consistency:** Results become tangible around Level 2 when you begin documenting processes and selecting the tools they run on.

Standardizing data formats, naming conventions, and processes so that the entire team always works off the same page. **Level 3 is when Consistency gets amplified as organized data unlocks analytics and reporting for scale.**

- **Clarity**: Gaining real-time visibility and accurate reporting across every department to make quick, informed decisions. **Level 3 is when Clarity occurs.** Unified data removes the need for copy/pasting and data duplication between tools and teams.

- **Capacity**: Freeing up human effort and resources, allowing you to handle more work (and bigger opportunities) with the same headcount. You will see some benefits at Level 3 from data automation, but **major gains in capacity come with workflow automation at Level 4.**

3 Cs	People	Process	Tools
Consistency Level 2	Team follows standard practices	Documented steps eliminate variation	Systems enforce data standards
Clarity Level 3	Everyone sees the same information	Regular reporting rituals	Real-time dashboards and alerts
Capacity Level 4+	Focus shifts to high-value work	Unnecessary steps eliminated	Automation handles routine tasks

Let's dive into each a bit deeper...

Consistency in Action

If your team uses standardized naming conventions, documented processes, and a central data repository, your daily operations become much smoother.

- **Reduced Errors**: A single source of truth eliminates duplication and guesswork.
- **Faster Tasks**: Teams don't waste time hunting for correct data or re-entering the same info in different places.
- **Scalable Processes**: When everyone follows the same steps, onboarding is faster and you can grow without chaos.

Documentation

When documentation is consistent, everyone follows the same playbook. A new customer signs up and they get the exact same onboarding experience regardless of which team member helps them.

When it's not, your best account manager leaves and takes their "special way" of handling VIP clients with them leaving you scrambling.

Client Example: A manufacturing client implemented standardized work instructions with visual aids for their assembly line. Error rates dropped in just one month, and training time for new hires decreased from two weeks to just 3 days.

Data

When data is consistent, customer names are formatted the same way across all platforms. No more "J. Smith," "John S.," and "Smith, John" for the same person.

When it's not, duplicate records multiply, reports become unreliable, and nobody trusts the numbers.

Real World Impact: Think about the last time you tried to filter a spreadsheet with inconsistent data formats. One meeting of trying to sort through irregular date formats (01/15/24, January 15, 2024, etc.) wastes everyone's time and erodes confidence.

Software

When software usage is consistent, everyone uses the same tools the same way. Fields are completed consistently, and integrations work reliably.

When it's not, some people use Slack for approvals, others email, and a few still walk documents around for signatures. Processes cannot be followed.

Exercise: Final Verification Checklist

Purpose: Create a simple "final check" list to ensure consistency before completing a high-value process.

Instructions:

1. Select one critical process in your business (client onboarding, order fulfillment, proposal submission, etc.)

2. Create a verification checklist of items that must be confirmed before the process is considered complete

Final Verification Checklist for: _____

✓	Item to Verify
	All required fields are completed
	Information is formatted correctly

✓	Item to Verify
	All attachments are included
	Approvals have been documented
	Client/customer has confirmed receipt
	Data has been entered in the system of record
	Follow-up actions are scheduled
	Quality check has been performed
	Pricing/billing information is accurate
	Delivery timeline has been communicated

Pro Tip: Laminate this checklist or create a digital version that team members can quickly reference before marking any critical process complete. Put it where the process happens, not a folder.

Clarity in Action

Once your data is consistently entered, you unlock the ability to see dashboards that update automatically, confirm stock levels without guesswork, or detect marketing anomalies quickly.

- **Faster Decision-Making**: Instead of "Let's meet next week when the spreadsheet is done," you can make calls in minutes.

- **Immediate Error Detection**: If sales data suddenly spikes (or plummets), you can investigate that same day.

- **Aligned Teams**: Everyone sees the same scorecard, so conversations focus on solutions, not debating whose numbers are right.

Documentation

When documentation creates clarity: Process maps show exactly where a customer order is in the fulfillment cycle. Anyone can quickly understand what's happening and what comes next.

When it doesn't: Teams become silos, with each department using different terminologies for the same concepts and causing confusion in cross-functional meetings.

Clarity Tool: Create a company glossary for your most important terms. When everyone defines "qualified lead" or "complete order" the same way, reports become instantly more valuable.

Data

When data provides clarity: Your executive dashboard shows real-time sales, production status, and cash position. Problems are spotted early, when they're still small.

When it doesn't: You discover a key shortage after promising a rush delivery to your biggest client.

Client Example: One of our service business clients implemented a color-coded dashboard showing which technicians were available in real-time.

Dispatch times improved by 35%, and customer satisfaction scores jumped 12 points in just one quarter.

Software

When software delivers clarity: Your CRM shows the exact status of every deal, with accurate probability forecasts, because everyone updates the system consistently.

When it doesn't: Sales managers spend hours in "forecast forensics," trying to figure out which deals are real and which are wishful thinking.

Exercise: Business Language Glossary

Purpose: Create a shared vocabulary that ensures everyone in your organization speaks the same language when discussing processes, systems, and metrics.

Instructions:

1. Identify terms that are frequently misunderstood or defined differently across teams
2. Define each term clearly and concisely
3. Categorize terms to make the glossary easier to navigate
4. Share with all team members and make it easily accessible

Categories to consider:

- System/Tool Names
- Process Terms
- Key Metrics
- Industry Jargon
- Internal Codewords
- Department-Specific Terms

Example Terms:

Term	Definition
Qualified Lead	A lead that meets our criteria of: [your criteria]
Sprint	A two-week work cycle where specific features are developed
CLTV	Customer Lifetime Value (total expected revenue from a customer)
Red Alert	A priority 1 customer issue requiring immediate response

Pro Tip: Review and update this glossary annually. Assign an owner who ensures definitions remain current as your business evolves. Add this to your onboarding process for new team members.

Capacity in Action

Capacity happens when teams no longer waste hours on grunt work. They can handle 2x or 3x the load by focusing on higher-value tasks while letting software handle the mundane.

- **Eliminated Busywork:** Automation handles repetitive tasks that once consumed hours of staff time.

- **Optimized Resources:** Data-driven decisions help allocate people and budget where they'll have the biggest impact.

- **Scalable Operations**: Growth doesn't require proportional hiring because your systems can handle increased volume.

Documentation

When documentation builds capacity: New hires become productive faster because they have clear guidance. New automation deploys faster too.

When it doesn't: Senior staff are interrupted to answer the same basic questions over and over.

Practical Tip: Document the 20% of processes that create 80% of your results first. Don't try to document everything at once. You'll never finish if you're growing.

Data

When data expands capacity: Analytics helps you staff appropriately for peaks without overhiring. You can see which products, services, or clients deliver the highest margins.

When it doesn't: You tie up resources (team, time, capital) that could be deployed elsewhere.

Case Study: A quick-serve franchise client automated their daily cash reconciliation across 50+ locations, saving 30 hours per week. That freed up a full-time finance employee to focus on analyzing trends instead of manual data entry.

Software

When software maximizes capacity: Automations trigger the right tasks to the right people at the right time. No more status meetings just to make sure work is flowing.

When it doesn't: Staff toggle between 5+ software tools to complete a single transaction, copy-pasting data between systems.

At **Level 4**, you're using advanced automation. That's where you can see a *massive* capacity leap, up to **10x** or more in some departments.

One of our manufacturing clients implemented a schedule system that factors in crew availability, location, and travel time to propose optimal daily routes, but only after they had reached Level 3 with clean, consistent data.

Exercise: Diagnose and Brainstorm Bottlenecks

Purpose: Quickly diagnose and resolve your most pressing operational bottleneck.

Instructions: Answer these questions about your biggest workflow bottleneck to uncover the right solution.

1. What specific process is currently backed up?

_____

2. Is this bottleneck...

☐ Approval-based (waiting for decisions)

☐ Capacity-based (not enough resources)

☐ Knowledge-based (lack of information/skills)

☐ System-based (technology limitations)

3. How frequently does this bottleneck occur?

☐ Constantly

☐ During specific peak times (which? _____)

☐   Unpredictably

4. Who feels the pain from this bottleneck most directly?

☐   Customers

☐   Employees

☐   Leadership

☐   Other: _____

5. Quick-win solution paths (check all that apply):

☐   Could approval thresholds be increased?

☐   Could approvals be batched instead of one-by-one?

☐   Could certain approvals be delegated to others?

☐   Could some approvals be eliminated entirely?

☐   Could parts of this process be automated?

☐   Could work be redistributed to other team members?

☐   Could you create templates or shortcuts?

☐   Could certain tasks be outsourced?

Action commitment: I will solve this bottleneck by:

_____

Target completion date: _____

The Executive Cs: Confidence and Cashflow

The 3 Cs create a powerful foundation for operational efficiency, but executives often care about two more Cs: **Confidence** and **Cashflow**.

- **Confidence** emerges when the leadership team sees reliable data and no longer feels one glitch away from chaos. They make bolder moves and spot opportunities earlier.

- **Cashflow** improves as inefficiencies drop and capacity expands. Fewer errors mean less overhead. Faster decision-making boosts revenue. A well-run digital operation translates directly into a stronger bottom line.

Digital Chaos Transformed: Two Success Stories

Let's check back in with Fitness Marketing Advisors to see the 3 Cs inside their operations.

Fitness Marketing Advisors: From Tool Overload to Streamlined Operations

Fitness Marketing Advisors took a different approach to their digital transformation. Rather than adding yet another tool to their tech stack, they focused on consolidating and creating a unified workflow:

Consistency: One Platform, One Process

They built a central platform with tailored workspaces specifically designed for each team's needs. Standard templates for client deliverables ensured everyone followed the same process every time. The longtime CRM, Keap, was integrated via API.

Communications became standardized, client expectations were consistently managed, and team members could seamlessly pick up each other's work during absences.

Clarity: Custom Dashboards for All

They created filtered views in the central platform to help teams manage their workload efficiently, based on project status, priority, and team member assignments. Everyone was now on the same page and could quickly get up to speed across all customers.

Leadership no longer needed to ask for status updates since they could see progress in real-time. Clients received consistent updates, and cross-department visibility eliminated redundant work.

Capacity: Automation of the Mundane

They implemented automations for routine tasks directly in the central platform. Task assignments, status updates, and deadline reminders happened without manual intervention.

The team reclaimed 40+ hours per week previously spent on administrative tasks and eventually managed to double their client capacity without increasing headcount.

Recap: 5 Levels + 3Cs

At **Level 1**, data is completely siloed and inconsistent.

- **Documentation** exists mostly in people's heads

- **Software** tools operate in complete isolation, often including paper-based processes

- **Data** is scattered and redundant with no standardization

At **Level 2**, you've laid groundwork but haven't connected systems.

- **Documentation** begins to emerge with basic process outlines and guidelines

- **Software** has moved to cloud-based platforms capable of integration (but not yet connected)

- **Data** standards are developing but information still requires manual transfers between systems

At **Level 3**, you have the foundation for dashboards, consistent processes, and the emergence of capacity gains.

- **Documentation** is centralized and standardized

- **Software** systems are integrated and speak the same language

- **Data** flows automatically between systems with minimal manual intervention

By the time you hit **Level 4**, automation will multiply your productivity utilize the foundation of Level 3.

- **Documentation** includes detailed process maps for automation

- **Software** triggers workflows automatically based on events

- **Data** is clean, validated, and trusted company-wide

If you try to plug an AI tool into a misaligned system, you'll just accelerate errors. That's why you must first address **Consistency** and **Clarity** as the bedrock for harnessing AI and automation effectively.

Key Takeaways

1. **Consistency:** This isn't just a nice concept. It's your gateway to drastically fewer errors and a smoother day-to-day.

2. **Clarity:** Once your data is consistent, you gain real-time insights. No more chasing down multiple spreadsheets or second-guessing your numbers.

3. **Capacity**: Free your team from mundane tasks, allowing them to handle more projects or initiatives without bloating headcount.

4. **Cause-Effect Chain**: Without Consistency, Clarity is impossible; without Clarity, you can't confidently grow Capacity.

When you get these 3 Cs right, the **Executive Cs** of **Confidence** and **Cashflow** follow naturally.

- In **Chapter 3**, we'll discuss the Foundational Pillars that create the backbone of Level 3 operations, focusing on Talent Strategy, Workflow Optimization and Digital Architecture.

- In **Chapter 4**, we'll explore the Advanced Pillars that take you to Levels 4 and 5, diving into Knowledge Management and AI Automation for exponential gains.

Why Bother?

Even a small step toward **Consistency** like picking a naming convention or standard input form can have a ripple effect. It reveals how much time you've been losing on rework and manual corrections. Once your team sees the payoff, they'll be more motivated to standardize additional processes. Over time, you'll have a consistent foundation across multiple departments, enabling the clarity and capacity leaps we've seen in countless client stories.

If you're feeling overwhelmed: **Consistency** first. You don't need every department to be perfect in a day. Start small, prove the results, and then scale it up. The path to advanced automation (Level 4) and AI (Level 5) rests on this vital foundation.

In **Chapter 3**, we'll explore the Foundational Pillars to systematically build these capabilities to eliminate the daily chaos that's been blocking growth.

CHAPTER 3

BUILDING TO LEVEL 3 USING
THE PILLARS OF DIGITAL OPERATIONS

The Invisible Digital Foundation

This story is painfully common. Organizations invest in cutting-edge tools, only to find themselves buried deeper in confusion.

Why? Because they haven't systematically built the foundational capabilities needed to support advanced technology.

The solution lies in developing what we call the 5 Pillars, the core capabilities that create a stable digital ecosystem and bring you reliably to Level 3 maturity -> then on to level 5.

Data Chaos in a Multi-Location Restaurant Empire

Our client had built an impressive operation of over 50 QSR locations along the West Coast. While their on site process was standardized thanks to corporate guidelines, their back-office operations were anything but structured. The franchise headquarters provided robust support for marketing, product sourcing, and operational SOPs, but left franchisees to fend for themselves when it came to financial systems and operations with dozens of stores.

This created a perfect storm of financial data chaos:

- **Scattered Communication**: Each location had its own method of reporting daily cash reconciliation. Some texted photos of register receipts, others scanned them, and still others emailed PDFs, all in varying formats and at different times of day.

- **Labor-Intensive Processing**: A full-time finance employee at headquarters spent virtually her entire workweek opening emails, downloading attachments, manually reviewing images and PDFs, and then transcribing cash totals into spreadsheets.

- **All-Hands Emergency Processing**: Once a week, the situation became so overwhelming that team members from HR would be pulled away from their regular duties for what they called "Receipt Tuesdays" to help organize and categorize the backlog of financial photos and documents.

- **Integration Nightmares**: The fragmented approach meant financial data wasn't properly flowing between systems. What should have been simple reconciliation became a complex detective exercise to find where discrepancies originated.

- **Delayed Financial Insights**: With reconciliation taking so long, the leadership team couldn't get a clear, real-time picture of their financial position. By the time data was processed, it was often too late to address concerning trends. Often up to 30 days later!

As the operations director described it: "We were stuck in receipts and blurry photos. We couldn't tell which locations were underperforming until weeks later because the data entry alone was consuming all our resources."

This level of digital chaos was creating serious Operational Debt.

The company had invested in point-of-sale systems, accounting software, and restaurant management tools, but the broken link between store-level cash handling and corporate financial systems undermined everything.

Without addressing this fundamental disconnect, they risked stunting growth and continuing to waste valuable human resources on mind-numbing data entry.

The Five Pillars of Digital Operations

While this chapter will focus on the three foundational pillars that get you to Level 3, it's important to understand the complete framework of all five pillars that support your digital operations journey:

Pillar	Components	Alignment
1. Talent Strategy	• Global team structure • Skills development • Training & adoption	People Foundational for Level 3
2. Workflow Optimization	• Process mapping • Documentation • Efficiency optimization	Process Foundational for Level 3
3. Digital Architecture	• System design • Data infrastructure • Tool integration	Tools Foundational for Levels 3
4. Knowledge Management	• Business intelligence	Process Advanced for Levels 3-5

Pillar	Components	Alignment
	• Process/Data standards • Prompt, SOP Library	
5. AI Automation	• AI tool selection • System deployment • Automation enhancement	Tools Advanced for Levels 3-5

In this chapter, we'll focus on the three **Foundational Pillars** (Talent Strategy, Workflow Optimization and Digital Architecture) that create the base for Level 3 operations. In Chapter 4, we'll explore the two **Advanced Pillars** (Knowledge Management and AI Automation) that enable progression to Levels 4 and 5.

The foundational pillars directly align with our **People → Process → Tools** methodology:

People (Talent Strategy)	Process (Workflow Optimization)	Tools (Digital Architecture)
Define clear digital roles and responsibilities	Map out step-by-step workflows to identify inefficiencies	Design an integrated system that connects your core software tools using standard APIs
Invest in skills development,	Document and continuously refine	Establish a central data infrastructure

People (Talent Strategy)	Process (Workflow Optimization)	Tools (Digital Architecture)
training, and digital adoption	processes through automation and improvement	and enforce data consistency standards
Create a culture that champions digital transformation	Remove bottlenecks with streamlined, repeatable processes and clear checklists	Ensure seamless tool integration to allow automatic data flow between systems

These three foundational pillars are precisely what enables an organization to achieve the 3 Cs we explored in Chapter 2:

- **Consistency** emerges from standardized processes and connected tools
- **Clarity** comes from unified data and visible workflows
- **Capacity** expands as integration eliminates duplicate work and enables basic automation

Let's explore each foundational pillar in detail.

Pillar 1: Talent Strategy

Goal: Build a flexible, digitally-capable workforce that's equipped and motivated to execute workflows effectively.

Systems that can talk to each other are nothing without who can operate them. Talent Strategy addresses who does what, how they're trained, where they're located, and how you ensure adoption of new processes and tools.

Key Components:

1. Team Structure

Organizing roles and responsibilities across your digital operations

What happens when it's missing: A manufacturing company had no designated owner for their overall digital systems. When problems arose, people pointed fingers. Sales blamed production, production blamed sales, and critical digital connections fell through the cracks.

Success example: A law firm created a "Digital Operations Specialist" role that bridged their legal, administrative, and IT teams. This person ensured new case management tools served everyone's needs and maintained data integrity across departments.

2. Skills Development

Ensuring team members have the technical knowledge to thrive

What happens when it's missing: A marketing agency purchased AI copywriting tools but provided no training. Most staff used 10% of the tool's capabilities or avoided it entirely, wasting thousands in subscription costs.

Success example: A manufacturing company created a "Digital Skills Matrix" identifying which team members needed training on which systems. They allocated 4 hours monthly for upskilling, resulting in staff becoming proficient in critical software.

3. Training & Adoption

Creating a culture that embraces digital tools and processes

What happens when it's missing: People continue using their preferred methods (often spreadsheets or paper), creating parallel processes that undermine consistency.

Success example: A financial services firm implemented a "Digital Champion" program where tech-savvy team members helped peers adopt new systems during office hours and coworking sessions. They celebrated small wins publicly and created friendly competitions, boosting adoption rates.

Culture Spotlight: Building Digital Confidence

Digital transformation often stalls because of cultural resistance, not technical limitations. Here's how to build a digital-positive culture:

- **Celebrate learning, not just mastery:** Recognize effort in adopting new tools, not just expertise

- **Make it safe to experiment:** Create sandbox environments where people can practice without fear

- **Connect to personal benefit:** Show how digital skills boost individual career prospects

- **Lead by example:** Ensure management visibly uses and champions digital tools

Assessment: Talent Strategy

Rate your organization on each component (1-5):

1. **Global Team Structure:** Have we clearly defined roles and responsibilities? _____

2. **Skills Development:** Do we have a plan to build necessary digital capabilities? _____

3. **Training & Adoption**: Are people actually using our digital tools effectively? _____

Watch Out For:

- Generational divides in digital comfort (requiring differentiated training approaches)

- Overreliance on "digital natives" without providing adequate process context

- Training without integrated application workflows and hands on opportunities

Practical Tip: For any major digital initiative, identify resistance leaders early and involve them in planning. Often the most vocal critics become your strongest advocates when they feel their concerns are addressed.

Workbook Reference: Check out the Role Template in the workbook's AI Automation Stages for the exact worksheet we use to document client roles for automation and optimization.

Pillar 2: Workflow Optimization

Goal: Create standardized, efficient workflows that eliminate mundane tasks, reduce errors, and free up creative energy.

With systems connected and people prepared, now you need clear processes. Workflow Optimization addresses how work moves through your organization:

- standardizing steps

- automating repetitive tasks

- continuously improving efficiency

Key Components:

1. Process Mapping

Documenting how work should flow, step by step

What happens when it's missing: A SaaS (software as a service) client relied on tribal knowledge for managing order changes. When a senior project manager left, the team lost critical process insights, leading to missed steps and unhappy customers.

Success example: A logistics company created visual flowcharts for their freight booking process. These simple diagrams reduced new hire training time from three weeks to four days and cut process errors.

2. Automation Design

Identifying repetitive tasks that can be handled by software

What happens when it's missing: Fitness Marketing Advisors team manually copied campaign data between their CRM, email platform, and reporting tools wasting 15+ hours weekly and introducing data errors.

Success example: An accounting firm automated client onboarding with document generation and e-signature tools. What once took 2.5 hours of manual work now happens in 20 minutes with fewer errors.

3. Efficiency Optimization

Continuously improving workflows to eliminate bottlenecks

What happens when it's missing: Inefficient approval processes. Simple decisions require multiple emails, meetings, or physical signatures, delaying projects by days or weeks.

Success example: A publishing team analyzed their content approval workflow and identified unnecessary steps. By empowering editors with clearer guidelines and removing redundant approvals, they reduced publication time by 40%.

Industry Variation: Workflow Approaches

Different industries emphasize different aspects of workflow optimization:

Industry	Primary Focus	Common Strategy
Professional Services	Billable time efficiency	Client intake automation, template libraries
Manufacturing	Error reduction	Visual work instructions, quality checkpoints
Healthcare	Compliance & safety	Structured protocols, verification steps
Creative/Marketing	Flexible collaboration	Kanban workflows, approval automation
Retail/eCommerce	Speed & volume	Order processing automation, inventory triggers

Assessment: Workflow Optimization

Rate your organization on each component (1-5):

1. **Process Mapping:** Have we documented our core workflows clearly?
   _____

2. **Automation Design**: Are we automating repetitive, low-judgment tasks? _____

3. **Efficiency Optimization**: Do we regularly review and improve our processes? _____

Watch Out For:

- Over-engineering simple processes with unnecessary steps

- Premature automation of unstable or undefined processes

- Workarounds becoming standard (indicating broken underlying processes)

- Tribal knowledge accidentally (or purposefully) held back

- Actually see how it is done, don't just trust the narrator

Practical Tip: Start with a process that generates the most complaints or errors. Map it out with the actual people who use it. You'll immediately spot improvement opportunities.

Pillar 3: Digital Architecture

Goal: Design an integrated, modular system that ensures data consistency and seamless handoffs between platforms.

Digital Architecture is your technological foundation

- how your systems connect

- how data flows between them

- how reliably they serve as your infrastructure

It's like the plumbing and electrical systems in a house: not glamorous, but if they fail, nothing else works.

Key Components:

1. System Design

Creating a blueprint for how your core software tools work together

What happens when it's missing: Western Siding had no coherent architecture. Sales used spreadsheets, production used an outdated ERP, and accounting used QuickBooks with no automated connections. When a customer changes an order, updates might reach one system but not others.

Success example: A healthcare provider mapped all their core systems (EHR, billing, scheduling) and identified critical data flows between them. This simple diagram helped them spot where patient information was getting lost and prioritize integration points.

2. Data Infrastructure

Establishing where key information is stored and how it's organized

What happens when it's missing: Fitness marketing Advisors stored client information in their CRM, creative assets in Dropbox, campaign performance in analytics platforms, and important decisions in email threads. Nobody could find a complete picture of any client relationship.

Success example: A professional services firm established their CRM as the "single source of truth" for all client data. They created clear fields for storing project requirements, budgets, and deadlines, eliminating duplicate and conflicting data.

3. Tool Integration

Connecting your applications so data flows automatically

What happens when it's missing: Staff at both the siding company and marketing agency spent hours copying data between systems. Information was often outdated or mismatched across platforms, leading to costly errors.

Success example: A retail business connected their e-commerce platform to their inventory system using Zapier, automatically updating stock levels when sales occurred. This eliminated 8 hours of weekly manual updates and reduced overselling by 74%.

Assessment: Digital Architecture

Rate your organization on each component (1-5, where 1 is "Nonexistent" and 5 is "Optimized"):

1. **System Design:** Do we have a clear blueprint for how our systems should connect? _____

2. **Data Infrastructure:** Have we established where critical data should be stored, formatted, and organized? _____

3. **Tool Integration:** Are our key applications connected to share data automatically? _____

Watch Out For:

- **Security blind spots** when connecting systems (always audit data access permissions)

- **Integration bottlenecks** where expensive custom development might be needed

- **Vendor lock-in** that limits future flexibility

Practical Tip: Start with a simple diagram showing your most important data flows (sales → production → fulfillment → accounting). Look for manual handoffs that could be automated, and note which systems act as primary records for different types of information.

From Cash Chaos to Financial Clarity

After recognizing that their financial operations were stuck at Level 1 (Information Silos), the Quick Serve Restaurant franchise took a systematic approach to transformation, following the People → Process → Tools methodology:

Talent Strategy Implementation

Before: One overwhelmed full-time employee plus borrowed HR staff for emergency processing.

After: They transformed their approach to finance team roles:

- **Redefined job descriptions** to focus on financial analysis rather than data entry

- **Trained staff** on the new automated systems and monitoring processes

- **Shifted mindsets** from "processors of data" to "analyzers of financial trends"

- **Created clear ownership** of the automated workflow with designated monitoring responsibilities

- **Freed up HR personnel** to focus on their actual responsibilities

Workflow Optimization Results

Before: Manual, error-prone processes with no standardization across locations.

After: They documented and streamlined their core financial processes:

- **Standardized reporting procedures** for all 50+ locations

- **Implemented OCR technology** to automatically extract data from PDFs and images

- **Created an automated pipeline** that processed documents and populated spreadsheets

- **Built in quality control checkpoints** with human oversight before final QuickBooks entry

- **Established notification systems** to alert the team of any anomalies or missing data

Digital Architecture Transformation

Before: Fragmented data collection with multiple input formats and no standardized system.

After: They implemented an integrated, automated system:

- Created a **unified inbox** dedicated to collecting financial reports from all locations

- Set up a **structured Google Drive** to organize documents by location and date

- Established **direct integrations** between their data processing workflow and QuickBooks

- Leveraged **an** automation platform to connect everything

- Integrated with their **central platform** for process management and oversight

Meaningful Results

Within just a few months of implementing these changes, the QSR group saw dramatic improvements:

- **30+ hours per week saved** through automation of manual data entry tasks

- **90% reduction in manual work** related to financial reconciliation

- **"Receipt Tuesdays" eliminated entirely**, freeing HR to focus on their primary responsibilities

- **Next day financial visibility** across all 50+ locations

- **Faster integration of new acquisitions** with a standardized onboarding process

- **Improved decision-making** with access to current, accurate financial data

As their head of finance reflected: "We went from spending all our time gathering data to actually using data to drive decisions. We can now spot trends across locations, identify underperforming stores quickly, and implement interventions before small issues become big problems."

Perhaps most telling was when they acquired three new franchise locations. What would have previously caused weeks of chaos during financial integration was handled smoothly within days as the new locations simply joined the established workflow.

This transformation didn't just save time; it fundamentally changed how the organization operated. By methodically building their Talent Strategy, Workflow Optimization capabilities and Digital Architecture they achieved not just Level 3 (Unified Data) but reached Level 4 (Automated Workflows)

This allows for faster integrations of new acquisitions, and more growth as a result.

Connecting to Levels and the 3 Cs

Developing these foundational pillars directly relates to the concepts we've explored in previous chapters:

The 5 Levels of Digital Operations

The foundational pillars take you reliably from Level 1 (Information Silos) through Level 2 (Connectable Cloud) to Level 3 (Unified Data):

- **Level 1**: Organizations typically have none of these pillars fully developed

- **Level 2**: Basic development of one or two pillars

- **Level 3**: All three foundational pillars functioning effectively together

From Chapter 2: The 3 Cs (Consistency, Clarity, Capacity)

Each pillar contributes directly to the 3 Cs:

Pillar	Contribution to Consistency	Contribution to Clarity	Contribution to Capacity
Talent Strategy	Well-trained teams following procedures	Clear understanding of roles and responsibilities	Skills to leverage digital tools effectively

Pillar	Contribution to Consistency	Contribution to Clarity	Contribution to Capacity
Workflow Optimization	Standardized processes	Visible status of work in progress	Elimination of unnecessary steps
Digital Architecture	Standardized data across platforms	Single source of truth for reporting	Automated data transfers

Summary: Key Takeaways

1. **Talent Strategy** ensures you have the right people with the right skills to operate your digital ecosystem.

2. **Workflow Optimization** establishes consistent, efficient processes that leverage your architecture and people.

3. **Digital Architecture** creates your technological foundation of connected systems with clean, flowing data.

4. **All Three Pillars Are Required** for Level 3. Focusing on just one or two will leave gaps that undermine your progress.

5. **People → Process → Tools** applies to each pillar: define roles first, document processes second, then implement or configure technology.

6. **Building These Pillars** is the prerequisite for the advanced capabilities covered in Chapter 4 (Knowledge Management and AI Automation).

Without these foundational pillars firmly in place, attempts to implement advanced automation or AI will only amplify existing chaos.

Next Up: Final 2 Pillars

Now that you understand the foundational pillars that get you to Level 3, we'll explore how to reach Levels 4 and 5 in the next chapter. We'll dive into the advanced technology pillars of Knowledge Management and AI Automation that build on this foundation for AI first digital operations.

Without mastering Talent Strategy, Workflow Optimization and Digital Architecture first, attempts to implement advanced capabilities will fail. Master the fundamentals, then reach for the stars.

CHAPTER 4

THE ADVANCED
PILLARS – REACHING LEVELS 4 & 5

"I hear people constantly talk about adopting AI and fancy automations, but I always ask them the same question: 'Do you have a solid data foundation to build on?' When they look confused, I know they're about to waste thousands on tools that will amplify their chaos rather than solve it."
- Michael Greenberg

The Next Evolution Awaits

We're entering the era of intelligent operations. Organizations that have established a solid Level 3 foundation now face an exciting frontier: leveraging Knowledge Management and AI Automation to achieve exponential gains in productivity and insight.

While Levels 1-3 focused on bringing order to chaos:

- unifying data

- documenting processes

- integrating systems

Levels 4-5 represent where your digital operations transition from merely efficient to truly intelligent.

Think of it this way:

Level 3 gives you a reliable car that gets you where you need to go.

Levels 4-5 give you a vehicle that suggests optimal routes and eventually drives itself.

In this chapter, we'll explore the two Advanced Pillars that enable this transformation, examine real-world success stories, and provide practical guidance for your own evolution to Levels 4-5.

The Digital PR Startup Challenge

Unlike most organizations that struggle through the lower levels, some forward-thinking companies build Level 4 capabilities from day one. One such example is a Digital PR startup that recognized the traditional podcast outreach model was fundamentally broken: Podcast Guest Launch.

The Traditional Challenge

Podcast outreach is incredibly labor-intensive. Based on experience from previous podcasting agencies (my first company was one back in the 2010s), the process typically required:

- Identifying shows that accept guests

- Verifying available contact information

- Assessing audience engagement

- Ensuring topic alignment

- Evaluating host compatibility

These tasks demanded enormous human effort. The most critical and time-consuming aspect was listening to episodes to determine show fit. Under the traditional model, a team member could only produce about 10 quality pitches per day, listening to episodes at double speed.

This created a brutal economic reality: a $15-20,000 annual client contract required one full-time staff member dedicated mostly to that client. The service was valuable but difficult to scale profitably.

> "The bottleneck wasn't our process, it was human capacity. No matter how efficient we made our team, humans can only listen to so many podcast episodes and craft so many personalized pitches. We needed to fundamentally rethink the approach."

The limitations were clear: each team member could only manage so many relationships, listen to so many hours of content, and craft so many personalized messages. Even with the best tools, human capacity created a hard ceiling on growth.

PGL faced a choice: follow the conventional path of hiring armies of outreach specialists, or build advanced digital operations from the ground up.

The Advanced Pillars

These advanced pillars require a second cycle of People→Process→Tools implementation, but with greater specialization.

1. **Knowledge Management** (Process): Transforming data into actionable intelligence

2. **AI Automation** (Tools): Moving from rule-based to intelligent systems

ADVANCED (Level 3 → Level 5)

- **People**: Data scientists, AI specialists, automation experts, product managers

- **Process:** Decision trees, predictive models, edge case handling, prompt engineering

- **Tools:** AI platforms, advanced automation, machine learning

Pillar 4: Knowledge Management

Goal: Integrate documentation, processes, and work management so every team member can find what they need quickly boosting consistency and collaboration.

Knowledge Management ensures that valuable information doesn't just exist in people's heads. It addresses how you document, share, and leverage organizational knowledge to maintain consistency and enable data-driven decisions.

Key Components:

1. Documentation

Recording important processes, standards, and institutional knowledge

What happens when it's missing: Organizations without centralized documentation develop inconsistent methods across teams and locations. When experienced staff leave, critical knowledge disappears with them, leading to quality issues and extremely lengthy training periods for new hires.

Success example: Companies that implement searchable knowledge bases with written procedures, video demonstrations, and troubleshooting guides see dramatic improvements. One service business reduced support resolution time by over 30% while cutting new staff onboarding time in half.

2. Business Intelligence

Transforming data into actionable insights

What happens when it's missing: Businesses struggle with manual reporting that takes days or weeks to compile. By the time insights are available, the opportunity to make timely adjustments has passed, and decision-makers rely on gut feelings rather than data.

Success example: Organizations that implement real-time dashboards showing key performance metrics enable proactive management. Team leaders can immediately identify trends, adjust resources, and optimize operations without waiting for end-of-month reports.

3. Process Standards

Establishing consistent guidelines for how work gets done

What happens when it's missing: Without standardization, teams create their own approaches to file naming, task management, and client communications. This creates confusion, duplicates effort, and delivers an inconsistent customer experience that damages your brand.

Success example: Businesses that implement standardized templates, workflows, and communication protocols see immediate efficiency gains. Many report 20-30% reductions in process time while simultaneously improving quality and compliance.

Role-Specific Perspectives:

Role	Knowledge Management Focus	Key Benefit
CEO/Owner	Strategic dashboards, competitive intelligence	Faster, data-informed decisions
Operations Leader	Process documentation, team guides, resource libraries	Consistent execution, easier scaling
Staff	Quick-reference materials, decision trees, coaching tools	Less uncertainty, higher confidence

Assessment: Knowledge Management

Rate your organization on each component (1-5):

1. **Documentation:** Do we have accessible, up-to-date documentation for critical processes? _____

2. **Business Intelligence:** Can we easily see and analyze key performance data? _____

3. **Process Standards:** Do we have consistent guidelines that everyone follows? _____

Watch Out For:

- **Documentation becoming outdated** as processes evolve

- **Data without context** that leads to misinterpretation

- **Overwhelming repositories** where important information gets buried

Practical Tip: Create "minimum viable documentation" for your three most critical processes. Focus on what's absolutely necessary to perform the task correctly rather than trying to document everything at once.

Pillar 5: AI Automation

Goal: Go beyond basic automation to leverage intelligent systems that enhance prediction, personalization, or generative tasks.

Once you've established solid capable talent, optimized workflows, digital architecture and reliable knowledge management, you're ready to supercharge your operations with AI. This pillar addresses how you select, implement, and enhance AI tools to dramatically expand your capacity.

Key Components:

1. AI Tool Selection

Choosing the right AI technologies for your specific needs

What happens when it's missing: Tools that don't integrate with existing systems or address their unique business needs. These implementations frequently become expensive shelf-ware that teams abandon after the initial excitement fades.

Success example: Companies that carefully evaluate AI tools based on their specific industry requirements and integration capabilities see dramatic returns.

2. System Deployment

Implementing AI in your daily operations

What happens when it's missing: Forcing staff to manually transfer data between platforms. This creates more work than it saves, leading to resistance and abandonment of potentially valuable AI capabilities.

Success example: Organizations that properly integrate AI assistants with their existing operational systems create seamless workflows. Customer service teams implementing AI systems for ticket categorization and response suggestions consistently achieve 40-50% improvements in response times while maintaining or improving quality.

3. Automation Enhancement

Using AI to expand your automated processes

What happens when it's missing: Many businesses implement basic rule-based automation that requires constant manual adjustments when conditions change. These rigid systems can't adapt to evolving business needs, creating maintenance overhead that diminishes their value over time.

Success example: Build "fuzzy logic" into your automations using LLMs and other AI tools to get beyond simple if this then that statements.

Assessment: AI Automation

Rate your organization on each component (1-5):

1. **AI Tool Selection:** Have we identified the right AI tools for our specific needs? _____

2. **System Deployment:** Are our AI tools integrated into our daily operations? _____

3. **Automation Enhancement:** Do we use AI to give automated workflows basic intelligence? _____

Watch Out For:

- **AI hallucinations** or errors from poor quality training data

- **Over-automation** of decisions that still require human judgment

- **"Black box" implementations** where outputs can't be explained or verified

Practical Tip: Start with a focused AI project that addresses a specific, measurable pain point with a single task. For example, use AI to draft follow up emails or categorize support tickets before tackling more complex applications.

The Progression to Advanced Digital Operations

The journey to Levels 4-5 follows a natural evolution rather than allowing random technology adoption.

The 5 Levels of Digital Operations

- **Level 3** provides the essential foundation of unified data and standardized processes

- **Levels 5** represents a qualitative shift from "efficient operations" to "intelligent operations"

Level	Talent Strategy	Workflow Optimization	Digital Architecture	Knowledge Management	AI Automation
1	Basic skills	Ad-hoc processes	Disconnected systems	Tribal knowledge	Minimal/None
2	Defined roles	Workflow Documentation	Cloud-based tools	Workflow Documentation	Minimal/None
3	Training program	Mapped processes to Systems	Integrated systems	Centralized resources	Targeted Use, Prompt Library
4	Digital proficiency	Automated Data Handling	Automated dashboards	Analytics insights	Process integration
5	Continuous learning	Optimized processes	Adaptive architecture	Intelligent reference	Comprehensive AI

The 3 Cs (Consistency, Clarity, Capacity)

- **Consistency** at Level 3 enables the predictable data patterns AI requires to learn effectively

- **Clarity** through unified data becomes enhanced by AI analytics assistants

- **Capacity** expands exponentially rather than incrementally at advanced levels

Foundational Pillars

- **Talent Strategy** evolves to include specialized roles like data scientists and AI engineers

- **Workflow Optimization** creates the documented processes that can be enhanced with AI

- **Digital Architecture** (Level 3) provides the integrated systems that advanced automation requires

Why AI Automation Requires Level 3 Maturity

Organizations that attempt to implement AI Automation without first achieving Level 3 maturity inevitably struggle because:

1. **Garbage In, Garbage Out**: AI systems trained on inconsistent or inaccurate data produce unreliable results

2. **Process Confusion**: Automating undefined or variant processes leads to unpredictable outcomes

3. **Skills Gap**: Teams struggling with basic digital tools cannot effectively leverage advanced AI capabilities

So many AI initiatives fail to deliver expected results because they're built on unstable foundations. The companies that succeed with AI don't just have better algorithms; they have better data, clearer processes, and more digitally fluent teams.

Comprehensive Pillar Assessment

Now that you've evaluated each pillar individually, let's see the complete picture of your digital operations capabilities:

Scorecard Summary

Pillar	Component 1	Component 2	Component 3	Pillar Average
Talent Strategy	Team Structure: ___	Skills Development: ___	Training & Adoption: ___	___
Workflow Optimization	Process Mapping: ___	Automation Design: ___	Efficiency Optimization: ___	___
Digital Architecture	System Design: ___	Data Infrastructure: ___	Tool Integration: ___	___
Knowledge Management	Documentation: ___	Business Intelligence: ___	Process Standards: ___	___
AI Automation	AI Tool Selection: ___	System Deployment: ___	Automation Enhancement: ___	___
Overall Average				___

Interpretation:

- **Scores of 1**: Needs immediate attention before you can progress to higher levels

- **Scores of 2**: Stable but needs implementation work to see real gains

- **Scores of 3**: You have a solid foundation but room for significant improvement

- **Scores of 4-5**: This pillar is well-developed and can support advanced digital operations

Summary: Key Takeaways

1. Level 3 is the Prerequisite: Advanced pillars require the unified data, standardized processes, and digital skills established at Level 3.

2. Knowledge Management Transforms Data

- Centralize institutional knowledge in accessible repositories
- Implement business intelligence dashboards for insight
- Create learning systems for continuous improvement

3. AI Automation Introduces Adaptive Intelligence:

- Enhance decision-making with AI assistants
- Automate complex content creation and analysis
- Implement capabilities for role based operations

4. Implementation Follows P→P→T:

- **People**: Develop specialized roles with advanced skills
- **Process**: Create automated workflows
- **Tools**: Deploy AI platforms for advanced automation

5. Exponential Capacity Gains Are Possible:

- Teams can achieve 5-10x+ productivity increases
- Organizations can scale without proportional headcount growth
- Resource allocation becomes abundant rather than restriced

6. Human-AI Collaboration Is the Goal:

- Humans focus on judgment, creativity, and relationships
- AI handles pattern recognition, repetitive tasks, and analysis
- The combination outperforms either humans or AI alone

7. Level 5 Represents Self-Optimizing Operations:

- Systems that learn and improve without constant human intervention
- Workflows that adapt to changing conditions automatically
- Organizations that can rapidly evolve in response to market shifts

Next Up: Digital Operations Roadmap

In Chapter 5, we'll explore how to implement everything you've learned through a structured roadmap. You'll discover how to sequence your digital evolution, set realistic timelines, avoid common pitfalls, and create a sustainable implementation plan that delivers tangible results.

We'll also examine how organizations successfully navigate the journey from Level 1 all the way to Level 5, with practical advice for every stage of maturity.

The roadmap will help you avoid the most common pitfall: trying to do too much at once. Instead, you'll learn to create momentum through focused initiatives that build on each other, creating a flywheel effect that accelerates your digital evolution.

Let's turn your digital aspirations into operational reality.

CHAPTER 5

LEVEL UP WITH
YOUR DIGITAL OPERATIONS ROADMAP

You've assessed your organization using our Digital Operations Self-Assessment in Chapter 1. You understand the 3 Cs (Consistency, Clarity, Capacity) that drive operational excellence. You've bought into the Five Pillars that support digital operations capabilities.

But now comes the hardest question: **How do you actually level up?**

In this chapter, we'll put together a step-by-step roadmap for turning the frameworks from previous chapters into tangible results. We'll explore timelines, common roadblocks, and the critical success factors from those that actually achieve it.

When Digital Aspirations Meet Reality

Consider the frustrating experience of **Fitness Marketing Advisors**, the marketing consultancy we met in Chapter 3. Before their successful transformation, they went through a painful period of digital stagnation:

- They knew their disconnected tools were creating inefficiencies

- They had already invested in multiple platforms, yet saw little improvement

- Teams kept creating workarounds rather than addressing root causes

- Every attempt to "fix things" seemed to add more complexity, not less

"We were drowning in tools but starving for results," their operations director told us. "We could see where we needed to go, but we couldn't figure out how to get there. Every attempt felt like we were just adding another layer of duct tape to a leaky pipe."

This is the implementation gap: the chasm between knowing what needs to be done and actually doing it.

The good news? There is a methodical path forward. Transforming your digital operations isn't about heroic overnight changes; it's about **consistent progress in the right sequence.**

The 4-Phase Level Up

The roadmap for every level is built from the same process

1. Grade and assess using the 5 Levels

2. Set achievable goals with the 3Cs

3. Break down required capabilities with the 5 Pillars

4. Assign and execute on the improvements

Let's explore each phase in detail.

Phase 1: Grade & Assess

Remember: Before you can improve, you must know where you stand.

Using the Digital Operations Self-Assessment, your first step is to honestly evaluate each department. This creates a "capabilities heatmap" of your organization.

Implementation Guidance:

- Assess each department separately, marketing might be at Level 3 while finance and operations are at Level 1

- Include team members in the assessment process for accuracy and buy-in

- Look for patterns and dependencies between departments

Common Pitfall: Many organizations overestimate their capabilities. Bring in an outside perspective if needed to ensure honesty. Being too generous in your self-assessment only sets you up for future frustration.

Pro Tip: Look for "Level 1" silos that directly impact customer experience or revenue. These should generally be addressed first unless they are fine total silos or very high investment (like shop/factory floors).

Phase 2: Set Achievable Goals

Once you understand your current state, set realistic quarterly and annual goals for improvement using the 3Cs and your current level as north stars.

Implementation Guidance:

- Focus on one level at a time, don't try to jump multiple levels at once

- Set quarterly rocks with clear success criteria (what "done" looks like)

- Prioritize Digital Architecture and Talent Strategy in earlier phases

- Use the 80/20 rule, there will be iterations

A full-time team focused on digital operations can typically handle 3-4 major improvement projects simultaneously. Don't overextend your resources.

Common Pitfall: Avoid the "big bang" approach. Trying to transform everything at once almost always fails. Instead, create momentum with smaller, successful projects that build on each other. North stars are for directional change, not phase shifts.

Level Up Planning Calendar (Example)

Quarter	Department	Current Level	Target Level	Priority Pillars
Q1	Sales	1	2	Digital Architecture, Knowledge Management
Q2	Operations	1	2	Digital Architecture, Workflow Optimization
Q2	Sales	2	3	Talent Strategy, Workflow Optimization
Q3	Operations	2	3	Knowledge Management, Workflow Optimization
Year 4	Marketing	2	3	Digital Architecture,

Quarter	Department	Current Level	Target Level	Priority Pillars
				Talent Strategy

Notice that we're not trying to improve everything at once. Instead, we focus on moving one department forward each quarter, with attention to the most critical pillars for that stage.

Phase 3: Break Down by Pillar & Department

Broad goals like "get to Level 3" aren't actionable. You need to break these down into specific initiatives within each pillar, customized for each department.

Implementation Guidance:

- Identify the capabilities needed within each pillar to reach the next level for each department

- Document dependencies (data and work) between departments, they normally map to the customer journey quite well

- Translate these into specific projects or initiatives for each capability underneath the relevant pillars

- Create a communication plan to keep everyone aligned

Common Pitfall: Beware of capability gaps greater than two levels. For example, if your Sale's team is on paper at Level 1 but your marketing is trying to implement Level 4 AI Automation with a new CRM, you're setting yourself up for failure. The foundation simply can't support advanced capabilities.

Example: Department Level Up Blueprint (Sales Level 1 → Level 3)

Rather than trying to implement everything at once, break your level up into focused capability projects. Each project builds on the others, creating a cohesive improvement plan:

Priority Projects

Project 1: CRM Implementation *(Digital Architecture)*

- Move from spreadsheets to cloud CRM system
- Launch initial deployment with basic functionality
- Establish standard data fields for leads and opportunities
- **Owner:** Sales Operations Manager

Project 2: Sales Team Digital Roles *(Talent Strategy)*

- Define clear digital responsibilities for each sales role
- Create accountability chart for CRM data maintenance
- Document who owns what in the sales tech stack
- **Owner:** Sales Director

Project 3: Lead Management Process *(Workflow Optimization)*

- Document lead-to-close process with standard steps
- Create visualization of sales pipeline stages
- Implement weekly pipeline review process
- **Owner:** Sales Enablement Lead

Upcoming Projects

Project 4: Email Platform Integration *(Digital Architecture)*

- Connect CRM with marketing email platform

- Ensure contact data syncs bidirectionally
- **Owner:** Marketing Ops (with Sales Ops support)

Project 5: CRM Training Program *(Talent Strategy)*

- Develop role-specific CRM training modules
- Create certification process for system usage
- **Owner:** Sales Enablement Lead

Project 6: Sales Collateral Repository *(Digital Architecture)*

- Establish central storage for all sales materials
- Implement version control and access permissions
- **Owner:** Sales Operations Manager

This project-based approach makes clear what we're focusing on NOW versus what's coming NEXT. It creates momentum through focused execution rather than trying to improve everything simultaneously.

EOS Tip: Each project should become a quarterly Rock for its owner, with regular Level 10 Meeting check-ins to maintain momentum and quickly identify issues.

Phase 4: Assign & Execute

The final phase turns plans into action through clear ownership and accountability.

Implementation Guidance:

- Assign a single owner for each initiative. When everyone is responsible, no one is
- Create weekly scorecards to track progress
- Establish a regular cadence of implementation reviews

- Celebrate wins and quickly troubleshoot obstacles

Common Pitfall: Don't underestimate the importance of change management. Technology changes are easy; behavior changes are hard. Plan for resistance and proactively address it.

Executing with IDS (Identify, Discuss, Solve)

When you hit roadblocks (and you will) use the simple IDS framework:

1. **Identify:** Name the specific obstacle blocking progress

2. **Discuss:** Explore root causes and potential solutions

3. **Solve:** Decide on a clear action plan with ownership and timeline

This pragmatic approach prevents implementation issues from derailing your entire transformation effort.

Case Study: Capability-Focused Digital Transformation at EcomGrowth Partners

EcomGrowth Partners, a rapidly expanding marketing agency rollup specializing in ecommerce clients, had grown to over 100 employees through acquiring six smaller agencies in just 18 months. While this acquisition strategy had rapidly expanded their client base and service offerings, it created significant operational challenges:

- **Fragmented Tech Stack:** Each acquired agency brought their own tools and systems.

- **Inconsistent Client Experience:** Client onboarding, reporting, and campaign management varied widely between teams

- **Data Silos:** No single view of client performance, team capacity, or financial metrics across the organization

- **Duplicated Effort**: Teams were recreating deliverables that already existed in other parts of the organization

- **Integration Struggles**: With each new acquisition, operational integration was taking 3-4 months, limiting growth potential

As the COO described: "We were great at acquiring companies but struggling to integrate them efficiently. Every acquisition meant inheriting another set of systems and processes. We needed a unified operations backbone."

The 6-Month Capability Transformation

Rather than attempting a complete overhaul at once, EcomGrowth Partners implemented a methodical, capability-focused approach to reach Level 3 within 6 months:

Month 1-2: Foundation Building

Project 1: Platform Selection & Architecture *(Digital Architecture → Consistency)*

- Evaluated and selected a well known software tool as the central operational platform
- Defined core data objects (clients, campaigns, deliverables)
- Created initial workspace structure for cross-agency organization
- **Result**: Core platform launched with initial functionality

Project 2: Cross-Agency Leadership Alignment *(Talent Strategy → Clarity)*

- Formed digital operations committee with leaders from each acquired agency
- Developed shared vision for unified operations + dashboard

- **Result:** Unified leadership commitment to the transformation

Project 3: Client Onboarding Standardization *(Workflow Optimization →
Consistency)*

- Documented existing onboarding processes from all agencies
- Designed standardized process incorporating best practices
- Created template automated form for consistent implementation
- **Result:** All new clients began following the unified onboarding process

Month 3-4: Integration & Expansion

Project 4: Campaign Management Workflow *(Workflow Optimization →
Capacity)*

- Mapped standard campaign creation workflow with stage gates
- Built automation for task assignment and notifications
- Created standardized naming conventions for deliverables
- **Result:** 40% reduction in campaign launch time

Project 5: Client Data Integration *(Digital Architecture → Clarity)*

- Connected the central operational platform with email marketing
  platforms and analytics tools
- Implemented standardized client reporting templates
- Created automated data flows for campaign performance metrics
- **Result:** Campaign performance visibility across all accounts

Month 5-6: Scaling & Optimization

Project 6: Capacity Planning Automation *(Digital Architecture →
Capacity)*

- Built resource allocation dashboard showing team bandwidth

- Implemented automated capacity forecasting for new business
- Created process for balancing work across teams
- **Result:** Balanced resource allocation and proactive capacity management

Project 7: Knowledge Repository Development *(Workflow Optimization → Clarity)*

- Centralized all agency intellectual property and deliverable templates
- Implemented version control and approval workflows
- Created searchable asset library for cross-team access
- **Result:** 70% reduction in time spent searching for existing materials

Project 8: Acquisition Integration Blueprint *(Talent Strategy → Capacity)*

- Documented 90 day integration kickoff for new acquisitions
- Created templated communication plans for acquisition announcements
- Developed training acceleration program for newly acquired teams
- **Result:** Reduced primary acquisition integration timeline from 6+ months to weeks

Results of the Capability-Focused Approach

By focusing on specific capabilities rather than broad pillars, EcomGrowth Partners achieved Level 3 digital operations within their 6-month target:

- **Reduction in errors** due to standardized processes and centralized data

- **Doubled client capacity** without increasing headcount through improved efficiency

- **Unified cross-agency visibility** with real-time dashboards showing performance metrics

- **Reduced acquisition integration time,** accelerating their growth strategy

- **Created scalable foundation** for Level 4 workflow automation across the organization

The CEO reflected: "Instead of trying to fix everything at once, we focused on the key capabilities that would drive the most value. By following a methodical sequence and building each capability on top of the previous ones, we created a transformation that actually stuck. When we acquired our seventh agency last month, they were fully integrated in just 8 weeks, which previously would have taken a full quarter."

Their successful digital transformation supported their aggressive acquisition strategy while simultaneously improving operational efficiency proving that with the right approach, organizations can achieve Level 3 operations even during periods of significant change and growth.

Common Pitfalls in Digital Operations

Even with the best planning, digital transformations face common challenges. Here are the top pitfalls to avoid:

1. The "Big Bang" Fallacy

The Mistake: Attempting to transform everything at once.

Avoidance Strategy: Iterative sequential changes have a much higher success rate than simultaneous transformations across multiple departments.

- Focus on no more than a few projects in a few departments per quarter

- Complete one level before starting the next

- Prioritize high-impact, visible wins early

2. Unbalanced Growth

The Mistake: Advancing one pillar too far ahead of others.

Avoidance Strategy: Develop in relative harmony. Your digital operations are only as strong as your weakest link.

- Keep Level gaps to no more than two levels
- If using advanced software, ensure your team's skills match its capabilities
- Balance technical implementation with process documentation

3. Ignoring People

The Mistake: Focusing solely on technical implementation while neglecting the human element. Assuming staff will naturally adapt to new digital systems.

Avoidance Strategy: Gartner research indicates that change management is the #1 factor in successful digital transformations.

- Involve future users early + often in the process
- Create clear "what's in it for me" messaging
- Provide ample training and support during transitions
- Budget at least 1 hour per week during transitions
- Create dedicated office hours for review
- Recognize and reward digital adoption

4. Perfection Paralysis

The Mistake: Waiting for the perfect solution instead of making steady progress.

Avoidance Strategy: Perfect is the enemy of good, especially in digital evolution.

- Adopt an 80/20 mindset.

- Implement "minimum viable processes" before perfect ones

- Plan for iteration rather than perfection on the first try

5. Neglecting Data Quality

The Mistake: Focusing on new tools and automation while ignoring the quality of underlying data.

The Reality: Poor data quality compounds through each level of your digital operations. Bad data = bad outcomes, no matter how sophisticated your systems.

Avoidance Strategy:

- Include data cleanup as a mandatory step in every system

- Establish data standards before major integrations

- Implement validation to prevent future data quality issues

Implementing Across the 5 Levels

Level 1 → Level 2: Foundation Building

Core Focus: Moving from disconnected tools to cloud-based systems that can eventually connect

Key Implementation Activities:

- Select cloud platforms with integration capabilities
- Document basic processes and data needs
- Establish naming conventions and basic standards
- Migrate critical data to new systems
- Provide foundational digital skills training

    Success Indicators: All critical business data stored in cloud platforms, basic documentation in place

Level 2 → Level 3: Integration & Consistency

Core Focus: Creating a unified data layer with connected systems

Key Implementation Activities:

- Implement API connections between core systems
- Establish data synchronization processes
- Create comprehensive workflow documentation
- Develop dashboards for cross-functional visibility
- Train teams on integrated workflows

    Success Indicators: Data flows automatically between systems, real-time dashboards operational

Level 3 → Level 4: Automation Acceleration

Core Focus: Reducing manual tasks through automation

Key Implementation Activities:

- Map processes for automation potential

- Implement workflow automations for routine tasks

- Develop more sophisticated reporting and analytics

- Train teams on automation management

  Success Indicators: reduction in manual tasks, consistent execution of core processes

Level 4 → Level 5: AI Enhancement

Core Focus: Leveraging AI for decision support and advanced automation

Key Implementation Activities:

- Identify high-value AI use cases

- Ensure data quality meets AI requirements

- Implement AI-enhanced workflows

- Develop human-AI collaboration models

- Train teams on working with AI systems

  Success Indicators: AI actively supporting decisions, handling complex tasks with minimal oversight

Implementation Insight: The journey from Level 1 to Level 3 is primarily about bringing order to chaos. From Level 3 to Level 5 is about unlocking exponential efficiency gains on that stable foundation.

Success Through Sequencing: People, Process, Then Tools Revisited

Remember the core principle: "People, Process, Then Tools." This sequencing is critical to each level up initiative:

1. **People**: Ensure roles are clear and skills are developed

2. **Process**: Document and optimize the workflow

3. **Tools**: Configure and implement the technology

The Western Siding Example:

When we met Western Siding, they were struggling with costly errors, order mistakes, and an inability to expand their sales team. Their successful transformation followed this exact sequencing:

1. **People First**: They clearly defined who was responsible for contract management, sales processes, and the production gateway. They established a CRM owner role to maintain data integrity.

2. **Process Second**: They mapped out standardized contract workflows, created clear guidelines for transitioning sales into production, and established a quality control process.

3. **Tools Last**: Only after roles and processes were clear did they implement the CRM, with a contract management tool configured to match their now-documented workflows.

The result? Dramatically reduced errors, successful expansion of their out-of-state sales team, and improved interdepartmental communication all without changing their core business.

Implementation Insight: When technology implementation fails, it's almost always because the people and process foundations weren't solid. The technology itself is rarely the problem.

Key Takeaways

1. **Follow the 4-Phase Process**: Grade & Assess → Set Achievable Goals → Break Down by Pillar & Department → Assign & Execute.

2. **Respect the Timeline:** A department typically needs 3-9 months to move up one level. Don't try to rush the process or skip levels.

3. **Balance Your Pillars:** Keep your capabilities within two levels of each other to avoid operational debt and integration issues.

4. **Sequence Properly:** Remember "People, Process, Then Tools" in that specific order, for every initiative.

5. **Manage Change:** Technology implementation is 20% technical and 80% cultural. Plan accordingly.

6. **Build the Flywheel:** The 3 Cs create a virtuous cycle that accelerates your progress over time.

Practical Exercise: Your 90-Day Level Up Plan

Let's translate what you've learned into immediate action with a simple 90-day planning template:

Step 1: Select Your Focus Area

Choose ONE department and identify its current level (1-5) for each pillar:

Pillar	Current Level	90-Day Target	Priority (H/M/L)
Digital Architecture			
Talent Strategy			
Workflow Optimization			

Pillar	Current Level	90-Day Target	Priority (H/M/L)
Knowledge Management			
AI Automation			

Step 2: Define Your Critical Next Actions

For your top two priority pillars, list 2-3 specific actions aligned to specific capabilities to take in the next 90 days:

Pillar	Capability 1	Capability 2	Capability 3
Digital Architecture	System Design	Data Infrastructure	Tool Integration
Talent Strategy	Global Team Structure	Skills Development	Training & Adoption
Workflow Optimization	Process Mapping	Automation Design	Efficiency Optimization
Knowledge Management	Documentation	Business Intelligence	Process Standards
AI Automation	AI Tool Selection	System Deployment	Automation Enhancement

Pillar 1: _____ 1. 2. 3.

Pillar 2: _____ 1. 2. 3.

Step 3: Assign Ownership

For each action, identify WHO will be responsible and by WHEN it will be completed:

Action	Owner	Due Date	Success Measure

Step 4: Schedule Implementation Reviews

Set a regular cadence to review progress:

- Weekly check-ins: Every _____ at _____

- Monthly deep dives: First _____ of each month

- 90-day assessment: _____ (date)

This simple exercise turns the concepts in this chapter into actionable steps. By focusing on just 90 days, you create momentum without overwhelming your team.

Final Thought

Digital transformation isn't a single event, it's a continuous evolution. The organizations that succeed are those that commit to a methodical journey rather than searching for magical shortcuts.

By following the roadmap outlined in this chapter, you create the operational foundation that not only improves your current performance but prepares you for whatever technological advances the future holds.

Remember: You can only reliably automate what you've first standardized and understood. Master the fundamentals first, and the advanced capabilities will follow naturally.

CONCLUSION

THE DIGITAL□LABOR REVOLUTION.

We opened this book with a simple warning: in a world where AI and automation are reshaping entire business models, plugging intelligence into a messy digital foundation turns into failed projects, flawed outputs, ballooning spend, and disillusioned teams:

What we call operational debt.

You now have the frameworks and the operating system to replace the hotfixes and half-done docs that make up that debt. Now, you can build a foundation for digital acceleration throughout your business operations:

- **5 Levels** to know where you are.

- **3 Cs** (**Consistency** → **Clarity** → **Capacity**) to set direction.

- **5 Pillars** to build specific capabilities that build the flywheel.

- And the sequencing that makes all of it work: **People** → **Process** → **Tools**.

The core principle remains non-negotiable: Discipline precedes scale.

AI is not a patch for operational chaos; it is a force multiplier for clean, well-designed operations.

Level 3, a unified data layer with standardized workflows and digitally capable teams, is your runway. From there, the Digital Operations Flywheel compounds: Consistency creates Clarity, Clarity unlocks Capacity, Capacity funds the next loop.

What disciplined action looks like

- **Time horizons:** Most SMBs under ~100 employees reach Level 3 in 6–18 months with focused effort. Moving a specific workflow or function from Level 3 to Level 4 can often be done within a quarter; company-wide automation takes longer. Level 5 (AI-powered operations) is sustainable only after this foundation exists.
- **Gap control:** Keep no pillar more than two levels ahead of the others. Imbalance creates debt.
- **Data rule:** Clean, enrich, then validate twice. Never automate dirty inputs.
- **Adoption rule:** Budget time for training and change management; technology without behavior change is theater.
- **Issue cadence:** Use IDS (Identify → Discuss → Solve) weekly to unblock progress.

Your next 90 days

1. **Run the assessment** (Chapter 1). Be candid.

2. **Pick one department** and one high-impact bottleneck.

3. **Apply the Pillars** (Chapters 3–4) to design the capability work; align roles first, document the workflow second, configure tools last.

4. **Execute the 4-phase plan** (Chapter 5) with single-owner accountability and weekly scorecards.

5. **Ship a visible win** and reinvest momentum into the next loop of the flywheel.

Next: The Tactical Appendices

The sections that follow are reference material to accelerate your path to Level 3 and beyond.

- **Case Studies Archive** For each case, capture: Start→End Level, pillar moves that mattered, 3C outcomes, and time to impact.

- **The Workbook:** Role Templates, process maps, checklists, standards, glossary scaffolds, and general advices from years in the field.

- **Level 4+ Whitepaper:** A practical path from automated workflows to agentic tools, agentic workflows, and, eventually, coworkers. For those already at Level 3 and beyond.

- **Risk & Compliance Roadmap:** Progressive controls that fit your level. Embed guardrails into workflows and architecture as you scale, rather than bolting them on.

- **First-Principles Project Planning:** The change-management and planning principles that turns frameworks into durable habits.

Final Advice

- **Follow the plan.** Steady stable transition over "big-bang" ambition.

- **Build the foundation.** Level 3 first, then build more advanced automation and tooling.

- **Conquer the digital labor revolution,** accelerate what is already working well in your operations.

Build the foundation, spin the flywheel, and prepare to conquer the digital labor revolution.

The next move is yours.

APPENDICES

THE ARCHIVE:
CASE STUDIES EXPANDED

Quick Serve Restaurant Franchise - From Cash Chaos to Financial Clarity

The Challenge

Our **Quick Serve Restaurant Franchise** client had built an impressive operation of over 50 stores along the West Coast. While their on-site processes were standardized thanks to corporate guidelines, their back-office operations were anything but structured.

The franchise headquarters provided robust support for:

- Marketing and brand standards
- Product sourcing and inventory management
- Operational SOPs for customer service

But left franchisees completely on their own when it came to:

- Financial systems and reporting
- Cash reconciliation and accounting
- Back-office workflows

This created a daily operations nightmare:

- **Manual Reconciliation:** Each location would email PDFs of their daily cash reports in various formats and at different times

- **Resource Drain:** A full-time finance employee spent virtually her entire workweek manually processing these reports

- **Delay in Insights:** Management couldn't get real-time financial visibility across locations

- **Error-Prone Process:** The manual nature of the work created numerous opportunities for mistakes

The finance team was drowning in reports and spending so much time just collecting data that they had no time left to actually analyze it and make informed decisions.

The Solution: Digital Architecture

1. Process Understanding Before Solution Design

We spent time with the finance team to fully understand their workflows:

- How reports arrived from different locations
- The exact data points needed from each report
- How the information flowed into their accounting system
- Where errors typically occurred and why

This crucial step demonstrated our commitment to solving their actual problems rather than simply implementing technology for its own sake.

2. Digital Architecture Implementation

With a clear understanding of their needs, we built an integrated system:

- **Unified Inbox:** Created a central email address dedicated to collecting financial reports
- **Structured Repository:** Established a Google Drive organization system by location and date

- **Integration Platform:** Implemented Make (formerly Integromat) as the automation backbone
- **Data Extraction System:** Deployed OCR technology to read cash amounts from PDF reports
- **Central Dashboard:** Built a Google Sheets dashboard to display all location data
- **Accounting Integration:** Connected the system to the accounting software for final data entry

3. Human First Design

We intentionally kept humans involved where it mattered:

- **Quality Control:** The finance team could review extracted data before it entered the accounting system
- **Exception Handling:** Staff could easily mark and correct any OCR errors
- **Regular Office Hours:** Established weekly drop-in sessions for team questions and feedback

The team appreciated that we took time to understand their processes before building anything. By watching them untangle the mess first, we were able to design a solution that actually worked for their specific needs.

The Results: From Level 1 to Level 3 Company-wide, Level 4 in Finance

The transformation took the franchise from Level 1 (Information Silos) company-wide to Level 3 (Unified Data Layer), with their financial operations reaching Level 4 (Automated Workflows):

- **90% REDUCTION IN MANUAL WORK (CONSISTENCY):** The standardized reporting format eliminated data entry errors and created reliable daily financial snapshots across all locations.

- **30+ HOURS PER WEEK SAVED (CAPACITY):** Finance staff were redirected from tedious data processing to valuable financial analysis and strategic initiatives.

- **NEAR REAL-TIME FINANCIAL VISIBILITY (CLARITY):** Management could immediately see performance trends across all 50+ locations, accelerating decision-making with trusted data.

- **FASTER ACQUISITION INTEGRATION (CAPACITY):** New locations could be quickly plugged into the existing system with a standardized onboarding process.

Key Takeaway

Digital transformation doesn't have to be complex to be powerful. By focusing on one critical process, daily cash reconciliation, this franchise dramatically improved their operations while creating a foundation for future enhancements.

Their journey demonstrates that reaching Level 3 company-wide, with Level 4 operations in finance, doesn't require a massive overhaul, just a methodical approach to solving real problems with appropriate technology.

Western Siding - From Siloed Systems to Scalable Operations

The Challenge

Western Siding had built a successful Siding manufacturing and installation business over 34 years, known for their quality craftsmanship in the region but struggling with operational inefficiencies that limited their growth potential. While their production quality remained excellent, their digital operations were fragmented and outdated.

The company had strengths in:

- High-quality custom manufacturing
- Skilled installation teams
- Strong local reputation for craftsmanship

But faced significant challenges with:

- Inconsistent contract management
- Disconnected department communications
- Error-prone order processing
- Inability to expand sales beyond their immediate region

This created a daily operations nightmare:

- **Fragmented Systems:** Sales used spreadsheets, production relied on an outdated ERP, and accounting used an accounting software with no automated connections
- **Order Change Chaos:** When customers changed orders, updates might reach one system but not others
- **Costly Errors:** They lost over $60,000 in a single year due to unsigned change orders
- **Tribal Knowledge:** Critical process knowledge existed only in certain employees' heads

The operations director struggled to maintain quality while scaling the business: "We couldn't expand our sales team because our systems couldn't handle the additional workload without creating more errors."

The Solution: People → Process → Tools Methodology

1. People First: Clarifying Roles and Responsibilities

Before implementing any new technology, the team focused on clearly defining digital responsibilities:

- Established clear ownership for contract management

- Defined responsibilities for the sales-to-production handoff

- Created a dedicated CRM owner role to maintain data integrity

- Identified who would manage the production gateway

2. Process Second: Documenting Critical Workflows

With roles clarified, the team mapped out standardized processes:

- Created a structured contract workflow with clear approval stages
- Established guidelines for transitioning sales orders into production
- Implemented quality control checkpoints at key handoff points
- Documented naming conventions and data standards

3. Tools Last: Implementing the Right Technology

Only after roles and processes were clearly defined did the team implement technology solutions:

- **CRM Implementation:** Created and deployed central customer database
- **Contract Management:** Integrated a digital contract handling tool.
- **Data Integration:** Connected their CRM with their production ERP and Accounting
- **Mobile Access:** Ensured field teams could access and update information remotely

The Results: From Level 1 to Level 3, Level 4 in Sales

The transformation took Western Siding from Level 1 (Information Silos) to Level 3 (Unified Data Layer) overall, with their sales operations reaching Level 4 (Automated Workflows):

- **ELIMINATED COSTLY ERRORS (CONSISTENCY):** Every change order and contract has been properly signed and tracked since implementation

- **ENHANCED COMMUNICATION (CLARITY):** All departments now work from the same customer data, eliminating misunderstandings and delays

- **ENABLED EXPANSION (CAPACITY):** Successfully expanded with an out-of-state sales team supported by their new unified digital system

- **IMPROVED CUSTOMER EXPERIENCE (CONSISTENCY):** Standardized processes ensured consistent quality regardless of which team member handled the order

Key Takeaway

Western Siding' transformation demonstrates that digital evolution isn't about implementing the latest technology. It's about creating a solid operational foundation that supports growth. By methodically building their digital capabilities starting with clear roles and documented processes, they were able to scale their business without compromising the quality craftsmanship that built their reputation.

Their journey shows how reaching Level 3 (with Level 4 in sales) enables expansion opportunities that weren't previously possible, all without changing their core business identity.

Fitness Marketing Advisors - From Tool Fragmentation to Streamlined Operations

The Challenge

Our **Fitness Marketing Advisors** client had bootstrapped impressively from a one-person consultancy to over 20 employees, helping gym owners and fitness trainers grow their businesses. While their industry expertise was strong, their digital infrastructure was creating significant inefficiencies.

The company excelled at:

- Marketing strategy for fitness businesses
- Content creation and campaign management
- Training and coaching for gym owners

But struggled with:

- Fragmented technology systems
- Cross-department collaboration
- Consistent client deliverables

This created an operational nightmare:

- **Tool Fragmentation:** Marketing, customer service, training materials, and communication happened in different tools with no central connection point.
- **Duplicate Work:** Teams were entering the same information across multiple platforms, wasting valuable time.
- **Cross-Department Friction:** Without a unified system, divisions struggled to collaborate efficiently. Marketing couldn't easily see what Sales had promised clients.

- **Inconsistent Client Experience:** Client onboarding and deliverables varied depending on which team member handled the account.

As their Operations Director described it: "We had all these fancy tools, but they didn't talk to each other. Our marketing team was spending half their day copying data between platforms instead of doing actual marketing work."

The Solution: Digital Architecture & Workflow Optimization

1. Process Understanding Before Solution Design

We began by mapping their entire client journey and internal workflows:

- How client information moved between departments
- Which tools were used at each stage of client engagement
- Where duplicate data entry was occurring
- Which processes were causing the most friction

This crucial first step revealed that adding yet another tool would only increase complexity. Instead, they needed consolidation and integration.

2. Platform Consolidation & Integration

Rather than layering more technology on their already complex stack, we focused on streamlining:

- **Central Platform:** Implemented their core operational hub with tailored workspaces
- **Process Templates:** Created standardized templates for client deliverables
- **CRM Integration:** Connected their longtime CRM via API
- **Custom Views:** Built filtered dashboards so teams could manage workloads efficiently

- **Automations:** Implemented automations for routine tasks like assignment, status updates, and deadline reminders

The Results: From Level 1 to Level 3

The transformation took Fitness Marketing Advisors from Level 1 (Information Silos) to Level 3 (Unified Data Layer) in just one quarter:

- **STANDARDIZED COMMUNICATIONS (CONSISTENCY):** Client expectations were consistently managed with standardized processes and deliverables.

- **40+ HOURS PER WEEK SAVED (CAPACITY):** The team reclaimed time previously spent on administrative tasks and manual data transfers.

- **REAL-TIME VISIBILITY (CLARITY):** Leadership no longer needed to ask for status updates, they could see progress in real-time across all clients.

- **DOUBLED CLIENT CAPACITY (CAPACITY):** The efficiency gains allowed them to double their client capacity without increasing headcount.

Key Takeaway

Digital transformation doesn't always mean more technology. Sometimes it means smarter, more integrated technology. By focusing on consolidation and creating a unified workflow, Fitness Marketing Advisors dramatically improved their operations while creating a foundation for scaling their business.

Their journey demonstrates that reaching Level 3 doesn't require complex enterprise systems, just thoughtful integration of the right tools with well-designed processes.

The Challenge

Our **Home & Commercial Services** client had built a successful business over 25 years, specializing in woodworking services. With 40+ employees, they had established a strong reputation for quality craftsmanship but were struggling with operational inefficiencies that were limiting their growth potential.

The company excelled at:

- High-quality woodworking
- Skilled craftspeople and technical expertise
- Strong customer relationships and reputation

But faced significant challenges with:

- Fragmented operational systems
- Inconsistent project management
- Manual quoting and billing processes

This created a daily operations nightmare:

- **No Central Operations System:** Various departments operated in silos with no unified way to track customers, projects, or communications

- **Missing CRM Functionality:** Sales pipeline management was inconsistent and tracking customer interactions was difficult

- **Project Management Chaos:** The process for initiating projects, assigning tasks, and tracking progress was disorganized, leading to delays and customer frustration

- **Manual Quoting Process:** They relied on an online form tool for quotes, which then had to be manually converted to invoices, with spreadsheets and email serving as intermediaries

The operations team was drowning in manual processes, spending more time managing paperwork than focusing on their core business strengths.

The Solution: Digital Architecture & Workflow Optimization

1. Digital Architecture Implementation

- **Unified Platform Selection:** Implemented the central hub for all operations

- **Custom CRM Configuration:** Developed a tailored CRM system to manage the sales pipeline

- **Integration Strategy:** Connected a form tool with the central platform and the accounting system

- **Automation Foundation:** Deployed an automation backbone tool connecting these systems

- **Reporting Infrastructure:** Created customized dashboards for real-time visibility across operations

2. Workflow Optimization

- **Quote-to-Cash Process:** Created a streamlined workflow from initial inquiry through quoting, project execution, and invoicing

- **Project Management Framework:** Established standardized project stages with role-based assignments and automatic notifications

- **Standardized Documentation:** Developed comprehensive SOPs in a common space

- **Custom Field Mapping:** Set up automations to populate the central platform fields from the automated form tool, including guided next steps for the team

- **Continuous Improvement Process:** Instituted weekly sessions to refine workflows and enhance integrated systems configurations

The Results: From Level 2 to Level 3 in Six Months

The transformation took the Home & Commercial Services company from Level 2 (Connectable Cloud) to Level 3 (Unified Data Layer) in just six months:

- **STANDARDIZED OPERATIONS (CONSISTENCY):** Established uniform processes for handling quotes, projects, and client communications across all departments.

- **REAL-TIME VISIBILITY (CLARITY):** Management gained complete pipeline and project visibility, enabling 30-60 day capacity planning.

- **IMPROVED PROJECT COMPLETION (CAPACITY):** On-time project completion rate increased dramatically, from under 70% to over 90%.

- **FINANCIAL IMPACT (CASHFLOW):** Achieved 5%+ increase in net operating income, translating to hundreds of thousands in additional profit.

- **ACCELERATED COLLECTIONS (CASHFLOW):** 80% improvement in collection speed through streamlined invoicing and automated reminders.

Key Takeaway

This transformation demonstrates that reaching Level 3 digital operations doesn't require a complete technology overhaul. It requires thoughtful integration and process optimization of existing systems. By focusing on Digital Architecture and Workflow Optimization, this 25-year-old company dramatically improved their operations while creating a foundation for future growth.

Their journey shows how a methodical approach to digital transformation can deliver significant financial returns in just six months, even for established businesses with long-standing operational practices.

Marketing Agency Rollup - From Disconnected Teams to Unified Operations

The Challenge

Our **Marketing Agency Rollup** client had rapidly expanded through acquiring multiple smaller agencies, creating a diverse team of over 100 employees specializing in e-commerce management, SMS marketing, email campaigns, and other digital services. While this acquisition strategy rapidly expanded their client base and service offerings, it created significant operational challenges.

The company had strengths in:

- Diverse marketing expertise across multiple channels
- Strong creative talent and industry specialization
- Impressive client portfolio across various sectors

But faced critical operational challenges:

- **Fragmented Tech Stack:** Each acquired agency brought their own tools creating a patchwork of disconnected systems

- **Inconsistent Client Experience:** Onboarding, reporting, and campaign management varied widely between teams based on their original agency procedures

- **Data Silos:** No single view of client performance, team capacity, or financial metrics existed across the organization

- **Integration Bottlenecks:** With each new acquisition, operational integration was taking months, severely limiting growth potential

- **Workflow Confusion:** Teams were recreating deliverables that already existed in other parts of the organization

The Solution: Digital Architecture & Workflow Optimization

1. Platform Consolidation & Architecture

- **Centralized Hub:** Implemented the core operational platform for all agencies

- **Workspace Structure:** Created a consistent organizational framework that accommodated different service types while maintaining standardized core elements

- **Data Modeling:** Defined standard data objects (clients, campaigns, deliverables) that worked across all agency types

- **Integration Layer:** Built connections to essential marketing platforms and analytics tools

2. Workflow Standardization

- **Cross-Agency Standards:** Created standardized workflows for client onboarding, campaign creation, and reporting

- **Status-Based Automations:** Developed automated task assignment based on workflow stages

- **Role-Based Permissions:** Implemented clear access controls and responsibility matrices

- **Project Templates:** Built reusable templates for common campaign types across all marketing disciplines

3. Capacity Management System

- **Auto-Assignment Engine:** Created a system that matched team members to tasks based on skills, availability, and workload

- **Resource Forecasting:** Implemented project pipeline visualization to predict future capacity needs

- **Balanced Team Management:** Developed "pod" structures that could flexibly expand or contract based on client demands

- **Acquisition Integration Blueprint:** Created a standardized process for onboarding new agency acquisitions

The Results: From Level 2 to Level 4 in Core Delivery Workflows

The transformation moved the Marketing Agency Rollup from Level 2 (Connectable Cloud) to Level 3 (Unified Data Layer) overall, with many core delivery workflows reaching Level 4 (Automated Workflows):

- **ACCELERATED TEAM INTEGRATION (CONSISTENCY):** New acquisition onboarding time dramatically reduced, allowing acquired teams to be productive within the larger organization much faster

- OPTIMIZED CAPACITY MANAGEMENT (CAPACITY): Resource allocation became balanced across the organization, eliminating both bottlenecks and idle time

- SIGNIFICANT ERROR REDUCTION (CONSISTENCY): Standardized processes and approvals substantially decreased campaign errors and delivery inconsistencies

- ENHANCED VISIBILITY (CLARITY): Management gained real-time dashboards showing performance metrics across all teams and clients

- DOUBLED CLIENT CAPACITY (CAPACITY): Teams were able to service substantially more clients without increasing headcount by eliminating duplicative work

Key Takeaway

This case demonstrates how digital operations maturity becomes increasingly critical as organizations grow through acquisition. By establishing a unified digital architecture and standardized workflows, the agency created a "plug and play" environment where new teams could be quickly integrated while maintaining operational excellence.

Their journey shows that reaching Level 3 overall with Level 4 in core delivery processes transforms acquisitions from operational headaches into strategic advantages, as each newly acquired team enhances rather than complicates the organization's capabilities.

WORKBOOK
(WORKSHEETS + TACTICAL GUIDES)

Workflow Documentation: Swimlanes, Flowcharts, and Checklists

Purpose: Map out an important workflow in your business to improve visibility and identify enhancement opportunities.

STEP 1: Select a Workflow

Choose any workflow in your business (working or not). Examples include:

- Client onboarding process
- Content creation and approval
- Order fulfillment
- Invoice processing
- Customer support ticketing

Workflow Name: _____

STEP 2: List People/Roles Involved

Identify everyone who touches this workflow:

1. _____

2. _____

3. _____

4. _____

STEP 3: Document the Step-by-Step Process

Step	Description	Person Responsible	Tool Used	Handoff To
1				
2				
3				
4				
5				

STEP 4: Create a Swimlane Diagram

Using your process documentation, create a swimlane diagram where each role has a lane and steps flow from left to right.

EXAMPLE: Blog Content Creation Workflow

People Involved:

1. Marketing Manager
2. Content Writer
3. Editor
4. Graphic Designer
5. Client

Process Steps:

Step	Description	Person Responsible	Tool Used	Handoff To
1	Create content brief	Marketing Manager	Google Docs	Content Writer
2	Draft blog post	Content Writer	Google Docs	Editor
3	Review and edit	Editor	Google Docs	Graphic Designer
4	Create supporting graphics	Graphic Designer	Canva	Marketing Manager
5	Final review	Marketing Manager	Google Docs	Client
6	Client approval	Client	Email	Marketing Manager
7	Publish and promote	Marketing Manager	WordPress, Buffer	-

Swimlane Diagram:

```
X[Marketing Manager] → Create content brief → [Content
Writer]
                                          ↓
                        Draft blog post
```

```
                              ↓
                          [Editor]
                              ↓
                      Review and edit
                              ↓
                     [Graphic Designer]
                              ↓
                  Create supporting graphics
                              ↓
                     [Marketing Manager]
                              ↓
                        Final review
                              ↓
                          [Client]
                              ↓
                      Client approval
                              ↓
                     [Marketing Manager]
                              ↓
                    Publish and promote
```
✕

Pro Tip: This exercise directly supports the Workflow Optimization pillar. Once you've documented your current process, look for:

- Steps that could be automated

- Handoffs where information gets lost

- Bottlenecks where work slows down

- Redundant approvals or checks

By visualizing your workflow, you'll often spot improvement opportunities that were previously invisible.

Introduction

- **Goal**: Provide a roadmap for rolling out new technology, focusing on adoption and long-term success.

- **Target Audience**: Founders, project leaders, implementers, and team members.

- **Key Focus**: Differentiating between the strategic role of founders and the operational focus of implementers.

Step 1: Foundational Planning

Founders' Role:

- Set a clear vision for the technology adoption.
- Communicate why the technology is important for the business's long-term success.
- Build alignment among the leadership team.
- Allocate resources for the training and adoption process.

Implementers' Role:

- Develop a practical timeline and roadmap for technology rollout.
- Break down tasks into manageable phases (e.g., initial pilot, full deployment, scaling).
- Assign key team members as "champions" for the technology adoption.

Step 2: Education & Training Strategy

Training Approach:

- **Office Hours**: Offer weekly "office hours" for questions and troubleshooting. This can be done by in-house experts or external consultants. It's essential for helping teams stay on track.

- **Recorded Training**: Create a series of videos covering the fundamental skills and knowledge required for using the new technology. These should be on-demand and accessible to anyone who needs them.

- **Workshops**: Schedule live workshops or "deep dive" sessions that cover specific use cases and best practices. Workshops can be used to provide hands-on experience and clarify concepts.

- **One-on-One Sessions**: Offer personalized, one-on-one sessions with trainers or experts for team members who need more focused attention or help with specific challenges.

- **Founders' Mandate**: Mandate that each team member must engage with the training materials. Block off specific time slots for learning to ensure the whole team is on board.

Step 3: Structuring the Adoption Process

For Founders:

- **Ensure Leadership Buy-In**: As a founder, ensure that your leadership team is fully aligned on the technology adoption process and can champion it within their teams.

- **Create Incentives for Adoption**: Tie performance incentives to the successful implementation and usage of the technology.

- **Track Progress and Provide Feedback**: Set up metrics to measure adoption progress and provide feedback loops. It could be in the form of team check-ins, usage statistics, or feedback surveys.

For Implementers:

- **Start Small, Scale Gradually**: Begin with a pilot group of users who can test the technology in real-world conditions. Use this group to iron out any issues before a wider rollout.

- **Support Throughout the Journey**: Use the office hours and workshops to support teams at each stage of implementation. Ensure that there is consistent support and a space to discuss issues openly.

- **Monitor Adoption and Provide Continuous Improvement**: Regularly monitor the technology's use, and ensure that training materials are being updated to reflect new features or common questions.

Step 4: Mandating and Reinforcing Learning

The Founders' Mandate: Ensure that learning and usage are not optional.

- **Time Block for Learning**: Implement mandatory time blocks dedicated to learning the technology, such as weekly or bi-weekly "learning hours."

- **Ensure Accountability**: Track progress and create accountability measures for team members who aren't engaging with the learning process. This could involve mandatory completion of a set number of hours or courses, or reporting on how the technology is being used in their role.

Building a Culture of Adoption: Foster a culture where everyone is expected to continuously learn and evolve with the new technology. Encourage team members to take ownership of their learning and share their insights with colleagues.

Step 5: Long-Term Support and Scaling

For Founders:

- Continue to emphasize the importance of the technology and innovation in driving the company forward.
- Scale support resources as the technology spreads across the organization.
- Celebrate successes and acknowledge milestones achieved by the team.

For Implementers:

- Offer ongoing support and check-ins, even after the initial rollout phase is over.

- As more people adopt the technology, develop a mentoring system where team members who are experts in the new tech can help others.

- Regularly update training and processes to ensure continued success and engagement.

Conclusion: Sustainable Adoption

- The ultimate goal is not just initial adoption, but sustained and effective use of the technology.

- With the right combination of training, support, and leadership, your company can not only implement new technologies but create a culture of continuous improvement and innovation.

Risk Mitigation & Regulatory Compliance

Why it matters and how to build it without overwhelming your systems.

This book focuses on building scalable, digital operations. Risk and compliance are critically important, but they're also highly contextual. A compliance checklist for a creative agency looks nothing like one for a healthcare SaaS company.

That's why we've placed this section in the workbook: to give teams a flexible but grounded approach to managing operational risk, especially in regulated or high-trust environments.

You don't need to be compliant with everything. You need to be compliant with what actually matters for your level, your industry, and your exposure.

Compliance by Level: A Progressive Approach to Risk Maturity

Risk and compliance maturity should evolve alongside your operational maturity. Trying to implement enterprise-grade controls when you're still running Level 2 workflows creates more confusion than clarity.

Use this matrix to align your compliance priorities with your current maturity level:

Level	Compliance Focus
Level 1 – Silos & Chaos	Minimal visibility. Focus on obvious vulnerabilities: unsecured data, undocumented access, and lack of ownership. Identify critical workflows and assign basic responsibility.
Level 2 – Connectable Cloud	Cloud introduces risk. Formalize who has access to what. Start tracking key documents. Write lightweight policies for data handling, approvals, and sensitive workflows.

Level 3 – Unified Data	With standardized workflows, embed compliance steps. Automate recordkeeping, track exceptions, and implement permissioning. Use audit-friendly tools and reliable documentation.
Level 4 – Automated Workflows	Automate compliance checks and alerts. Build in approval logic, anomaly detection, and exception-handling. Prepare for formal audits or certifications (e.g., SOC 2 readiness).
Level 5 – AI-Powered Ops	Govern automated decisions. Ensure traceability, fairness, and security in ML/AI models. Maintain audit logs for AI actions. Continuously monitor high-risk workflows at scale.

Pillars & Compliance

Use the 5 **Pillars of Capability** to assign ownership for compliance improvements:

Pillar	Compliance Touchpoint Example
Talent Strategy	Training records, defined compliance responsibilities
Workflow Optimization	Embedded checks, SOP alignment, exception handling
Digital Architecture	Secure access control, audit logging, versioning

Knowledge Management	Documented policies, evidence trails, audit preparedness
AI Automation	Risk detection, decision traceability, regulatory guardrails

Risk & Compliance Self-Check

Use this checklist to assess your current risk baseline.

People

- Roles with compliance responsibility are clearly defined
- Compliance training is documented and recurring
- Access control is role-based and updated regularly

Process

- Risk-prone workflows are documented (e.g., billing, contracts, data access)
- Exception paths and escalation processes are defined
- SOPs include compliance steps where relevant

Tools

- Core systems include audit logs or version tracking
- Sensitive data is encrypted, access-controlled, and backed up
- Vendor and API integrations are documented and reviewed periodically

Optional Team Prompt (Use in Planning Sessions)

- What level are we currently operating at (1–5)?
- What compliance scope is realistic and necessary at this level?

- Where are we overbuilding or under-protecting?

- Who owns each risk-related responsibility?

- What would "audit readiness" look like at our level?

Final Note on Risk & Compliance

You don't need to bolt compliance onto the side of your business. You can build it into your operations as you grow.

In most companies, operational risk isn't caused by bad actors. It's caused by inconsistency, confusion, and invisible processes, the very things the Digital Operations Framework is designed to fix.

If you focus on the right controls at the right time and align them to your maturity, you'll build trust, resilience, and audit-readiness without losing speed.

First Principles of Project Planning

Why Project Planning?

1. Why is this good and key for LE

2. Why do we need a common language

3. What is the key use for this sort of planning?

What Is a Project?

A project is work that needs to be done. It has an end deliverable, which means that you are working to create something - either a tangible product, specific vision, or an effect.

All projects can be defined in two ways as either Fixed Term or Marathons. If you have not managed to place your project in one of the two categories, you have not defined it well enough.

Fixed Term

Fixed Terms could be considered as a sprint. They generally tend to have a defined endpoint, and could include:

● Creating a website
● Identifying 50 new potential suppliers
● Baking a Cake
● Launching a business in 30 days

Marathons

Marathons could be considered as an endless series. The idea that Marathons stem is the fact that it is a repeating set of tasks that you want to do for pretty much forever. A few examples of what can be considered as Marathon projects are:

● Sales
● Ad Management
● Bookkeeping

Rhythm

Rhythm is the timespan upon which a project is tracked. I generally operate on a weekly rhythm for projects, but plan on a monthly or quarterly basis.

Paced (Sprints)

A paced rhythm is when you have a certain amount of time available along with a list of tasks that need to be done. Each period you try to complete as much as possible, then reassign and review accordingly.

Marathon projects are often paced loops or sprints.

Mandated

A mandated rhythm is when you have a set amount of time to complete something and must send it out into the world at the end of that time. This could be "every 30 days we ship a new feature" or it could be "we have to deliver this client report on Friday" - a deadline is a deadline when we are planning.

It has to be done on time. Therefore, we will start reducing to just the requirements so that it can be completed on time.

Budgets

There are only two true categories of resources. Time and Capital - I use Capital instead of "Money" here to include Social and other sorts of relational capital in the same category.

If you want to set the budget, you need to have a general idea of the amount of time it might take to get things done.

In most cases, you can substitute time for money by doing it yourself. You can substitute money for time in almost every case by hiring others.

Budgeting is key to long term success. It allows us to work on multiple projects at once and efficiently allocate resources to achieve our goals.

Time

Time refers to the actual hours you or your team have to dedicate to a specific project or task. People have a limited amount of time in their day. It includes mandated project deadlines and milestones.

Money

Money allows you to purchase things, including other people's time.

Leads, Coordinators, and Strategists

Every team will have an assigned Lead, who is their functional head. They are normally the most senior and experienced team member

Most teams also have an assigned Project Manager, often designated by a coordinator or producer role. They make sure that things will be completed on time, that the project is updated in any management tools, and that all work is assigned properly and without delay.

Finally, a team may have a strategist or analyst assigned as well. Strategists provide Subject Matter Expertise to the team outside the bounds of the Lead's knowledge.

Roles

Roles pertain to a particular project. They are not titles in the traditional sense, but designations of responsibility.

When you first design a project, one of the best things you can try to do is map out the different skill sets involved and categorize them into roles that can be assigned to individuals.

In the creation of this document. I employ a separate writer's assistant whose job is to interview me, categorize my thoughts, and to expand and research upon subjects as needed. Thus, I have created a distinct role that I can dedicate resources into, which does include my own bandwidth - because my bandwidth is limited.

Bandwidth

Bandwidth is the idea that people will have limited amounts of time and thought. Therefore, they can only take on so many tasks and take on so many roles. People have a very limited amount of bandwidth. Most cannot handle more than a few roles. The amount of time available often drops by 10-20% per role due to context switching.

Personally, I see my own productivity drop steeply beyond 2 or 3 active projects.

For example, a freelance writer handles all roles when they start operating as their own business:

● Business Development - Finding and pitching new clients
● Account Management - Onboarding new clients, handling billing and invoicing
● Project Management - Developing project plans, timelines, and milestones
● Content Creation - Actually doing the work for clients like writing, design, development, etc.

As the bandwidth required for each role grows, the freelancer begins delegating these roles to new team members and grows into an agency:

● Business Development Manager
● Account Coordinator
● Project Manager
● Content Creators

As the freelancer builds a team, each new hire is focused on a single specialized role. The Business Development Manager develops leads, the Account Coordinator handles specific client accounts, the Project Manager develops timelines for their assigned projects, and the Content Creators focus on their particular skill like writing, design, or development.

Most mature companies follow this structure, with each employee having a clearly-defined and focused role so they can become highly specialized experts in their field.

Estimating Projects

Estimation refers to the amount of time it would take to complete a project or task. We start with time before converting to money because we must be attempt to estimate the work ourselves so we can improve our project planning abilities. If you are not an expert in a craft, do not rely upon your own estimate.

Triple It

The simplest way to estimate the time it would take on a project is to take your initial instinct and triple it. Your initial estimate will almost always be too short. Tripling it will create conservative time estimates that are more likely to be accurate or overestimated. It is better to overestimate than to underestimate when it comes to timelines.

Hours, Points, or Tasks

When managing projects and tasks within a team, it is essential to consider the most effective method for measuring progress and assigning work. There are various ways to do this, including tracking hours, using sprint points, or focusing on discrete tasks. Each method has its pros and cons, and the best approach will depend on your team's specific needs and working style.

Hours/Time Pro/Con

Pros:

1. Easily understood by both team members and clients.
2. Provides a clear basis for billing clients in agency settings.
3. Allows for accurate time and cost estimation for projects.

Cons:

1. Can be demotivating for team members if they feel they are being micromanaged.
2. Time-tracking can be seen as an administrative burden.
3. May not be suitable for flexible, creative, or innovative projects where time spent is not directly correlated with value produced.

Sprint Points/Poker Pro/Con

Pros:

1. Encourages collaboration and team input in task estimation.
2. Allows for more accurate project planning and resource allocation.
3. Can provide a better measure of the complexity or difficulty of tasks, rather than just time spent.

Cons:

1. Requires team members to be familiar with the sprint points system and the estimation process.
2. Can be difficult to translate into billable hours for client-facing projects.

3. May lead to confusion or disagreements around point values and estimation accuracy.

Kanban/Discrete Tasks Pro/Con

Pros:

1. Provides a clear visual representation of work progress and task status.
2. Can be easily adapted to different team sizes and project types.
3. Encourages a focus on continuous improvement and process efficiency.

Cons:

1. May not provide a clear basis for billing clients in agency settings.
2. Can be difficult to estimate project timelines or resource allocation without additional planning tools.
3. May lead to a focus on completing tasks quickly, rather than delivering high-quality results.

Our Path from No time -> Timed -> Points -> Journal

1. **No time:** Initially, the team operates without any formal time tracking or task estimation methods. This approach may work for small teams or projects with a flexible timeline, but it can lead to inefficiencies and difficulties in managing workloads.

2. **Timed:** To improve project planning and client billing, the team introduces time tracking for all tasks. This allows for more accurate cost and resource estimation, but may also create administrative burdens and potential demotivation for team members.

3. **Points:** The team transitions to using sprint points to estimate task complexity and difficulty, rather than just time spent. This encourages collaboration and provides better insight into project progress, but may

require additional training and adaptation for team members and clients.

4. **Journal:** Transition to public work journals and standups

Mise En Place (Everything in place)

Mise En Place is a fantastic project management concept. It refers to the practice of everything being laid out before a chef starts cooking. If you use this within a business, it forces you to start out with a better understanding of what must be done. This will prevent you from making simple mistakes.

Good chefs will read the recipes before they start. Similarly, a project manager should know everything that needs to be done. You should know what needs to be done before the project starts with your research and planning.

Priority, Micro Edition

The easy way to think about Mise En Place is with a mandated project of fixed term. It is vital that you chart out beforehand what parts of the project need to be done in order for it to accomplish its goal and what parts of the project should be done for it to do it best.

If something comes up, you can abandon the less important components to get it shipped on time. Without a clear plan and list, you will have no idea what is critical and what can be abandoned.

You should plan backwards from your end result. If a project is estimated at 120 hours, you can't plan to start just 2 weeks out.

ADVANCED WHITEPAPER (LEVEL 4+): THE 4-STAGE AI IMPLEMENTATION ROADMAP

A systematic framework for building business-ready AI capabilities

AI tools that function like dependable team members (and not science projects) require strategic implementation. This roadmap shows you how to build from simple automation toward true AI coworkers that handle complex processes autonomously.

At-a-Glance: The 4 Stages

Each stage builds directly on its predecessor, creating a foundation for increasingly sophisticated capability:

Stage	Autonomy Level	What It Does	Business Value	Implementation Complexity
1: Automated Workflows	None	Eliminates repetitive tasks	Time savings	Low (Existing tools)
2: Agentic Tools	Intern	Makes decisions within	Improved quality + speed	Medium (AI

Stage	Autonomy Level	What It Does	Business Value	Implementation Complexity
		defined scopes		components)
3: Agentic Workflows	Specialist	Coordinates multiple tools across entire processes	Capacity transformation	High (System integration)
4: Drop-in AI Coworkers	Peer	Functions alongside humans managers	Organizational scaling	Very High (Full stack AI)

Key Implementation Principle: Start with Stage 1 automation using tools you already have, while simultaneously investing in Stage 2 microservices for key processes. This is why documenting all loops/tasks in a role during Stage 1 is critical - it creates the foundation for targeted AI development.

Selecting the Right AI System: Implementation Decision Framework

The most effective AI implementations match system complexity to business process requirements. This framework helps you determine whether to implement a Task-Specific Microservice (Stage 2), Agentic Workflow (Stage 3), or AI Coworker (Stage 4).

System Comparison Matrix

Decision Factor	Task-Specific Microservices (Stage 2)	Agentic Workflows (Stage 3)	Drop-in AI Coworkers (Stage 4)
Process Scope	Single focused task (<3 Prompts)	Complete process with multiple components	Entire responsibility area or role
Implementation Complexity	Days or Weeks	Weeks or Months	Months
Human Involvement	Initiation, Direction, and Review	Initiation, Approval Checkpoints	Periodic oversight and direction
Adaptability	Limited to defined parameters	Process-aware with some adaptation	High adaptability across varying conditions
Capital Investment	Low to moderate	Moderate to high	High
Maintenance Requirements	Minimal, focused updates	Regular component coordination	Ongoing strategic alignment
Example Tasks	• Content generation • Data processing	• Client onboarding • Content Calender	• Executive assistant • Customer support

Decision Factor	Task-Specific Microservices (Stage 2)	Agentic Workflows (Stage 3)	Drop-in AI Coworkers (Stage 4)
	• Research briefs	• Sales Report Q&A	• Content manager • Research analyst

When to Use Each System Type

Stage 2: Task-Specific Microservices

- **Best for:** Well-defined, repeatable tasks that require some judgment
- **Business value:** Quick wins with minimal investment and immediate ROI
- **Implementation approach:** Start with high-frequency, routine tasks that create bottlenecks
- **Key advantage:** Flexible deployment across multiple interfaces (Slack, email, web app)

Stage 3: Agentic Workflows

- **Best for:** Multi-step processes requiring coordination between different specialized functions
- **Business value:** End-to-end process transformation with strategic human input
- **Implementation approach:** Build from proven Stage 2 components with well-documented interfaces
- **Key advantage:** Maintains critical human judgment while automating routine execution steps

Stage 4: Drop-in AI Coworkers

- **Best for:** Complex roles where full context understanding creates significant advantage
- **Business value:** Role fulfillment with minimal ongoing management
- **Implementation approach:** Evolve from successful Stage 3 workflows with expanded KOODAR framework
- **Key advantage:** Autonomous operation with professional-level quality and adaptability

Implementation Pathway Best Practices

1. Start with Stage 2 for rapid ROI

- Task-Specific Microservices provide immediate value with minimal investment
- They create building blocks for more advanced implementations
- Their flexibility allows deployment across multiple interfaces and workflows

2. Progress to Stage 3 when coordinating multiple components

- Combine proven Stage 2 microservices into coherent workflows
- Maintain human checkpoints at strategic decision points
- Document process flows and exception handling thoroughly

3. Advance to Stage 4 only for high-value, complex roles

- Complete KOODAR implementation with all six capability areas
- Ensure robust monitoring and performance evaluation systems
- Start with well-defined roles before attempting more ambiguous ones

4. Maintain hybrid approach for optimal results

- Not every process needs to advance to Stage 4

- Many businesses operate most efficiently with a mix of Stage 2 and 3 systems
- Focus advanced implementations where autonomy creates clear competitive advantage

Remember: Each stage builds upon previous capabilities while adding new layers of sophistication. The goal is not to reach Stage 4 for every process, but to apply the right level of capability to each business need.

Stage 1: Automated Workflows

Start with what you already have to build momentum

Before investing in complex AI systems, identify and automate repetitive tasks using your existing tools. This creates immediate ROI while laying the groundwork for more advanced capabilities.

Characteristics:

- Clearly defined triggers and actions
- Rule-based decision paths
- Minimal or no autonomy
- Highly predictable outcomes

Role Template (First Step):

```
X#### Role Name
The goal of this role is to....

#### Objectives + Metrics

#### Role Responsibilities

Quarterly
```

```
- List quarterly tasks

Monthly
- List monthly tasks

Weekly
- List weekly tasks

Daily
- List daily tasks

Triggered Tasks
- List event-based tasks

Infinite Tasks
- List ongoing responsibilities
```
✕

Implementation Strategy:

1. Document all tasks using the role template above

- Be comprehensive - capture everything the role does
- Note time spent on each task category
- Identify which tasks are repetitive vs. creative/strategies

2. Look for automation within existing platforms first

- Most CRMs have built-in automation rules
- Project management tools often include workflow automation
- Email platforms typically offer sequence/follow-up capabilities
- Leverage what you're already paying for before adding new tools

3. Then explore no-code automation tools for cross-platform needs

- Zapier, Make, N8N for connecting different systems
- Microsoft Power Automate for Office/Teams environments

- Workato for enterprise-grade integrations

4. Prioritize automation candidates by:

- Frequency (daily tasks before monthly ones)
- Volume (high-occurrence tasks before rare exceptions)
- Error impact (tasks where mistakes are costly)
- Time consumption (tasks that take significant human time)

Common Stage 1 Automation Examples:

1. CRM-Based Automations:

- Automatic follow-up emails based on lead status changes
- Task creation when deals reach specific stages
- Contact record updates based on form submissions
- Automated reporting and dashboard updates

2. Project Management Automations:

- Task assignments based on project templates
- Status updates when files are uploaded or approved
- Deadline reminders and escalation protocols
- Resource allocation notifications

3. Communication Automations:

- Meeting scheduling and calendar management
- Standard response templates for common inquiries
- Document generation from structured data
- Cross-posting content between platforms

Stage 2: Agentic Tools (Task-Specific Microservices)

Your lowest-friction entry point to AI adoption

Stage 2 introduces individual AI tools, often built as microservices, that possess a degree of autonomy. Unlike Stage 1's rule-based triggers, these tools exhibit:

- **Autonomous decision-making** within a defined scope.
- **Goal-oriented behavior** to achieve specific outcomes.
- **Adaptability and basic reasoning capabilities** to handle variations.

A practical and effective way to implement these is through **task-specific microservices**: specialized AI components designed to perform exactly one task with a defined input and output. This approach offers key advantages like **simplicity** (easy to develop, test, maintain), **compatibility** (easy integration), and **incremental scalability** (start small, add more later).

The Microservice Formula:

1 Input + 1 Process + 1 Output = Focused Value

```
Xgraph LR
    A[Input: Single Data Point] --> B[Process: 1-3 LLM
Functions]
    B --> C[Output: Single Result]
X
```

Key Advantage: Interface Flexibility

The same underlying microservice logic can be accessed through various interfaces, maximizing its utility across different teams and workflows. This means the core capability can be used by AI agents in larger workflows, integrated directly into tools (like a CRM plugin), or used manually by human operators via dashboards or chat commands.

```
X                       ┌──── Chrome Plugin
                        │
```

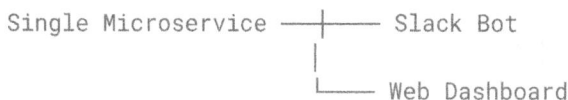

```
Single Microservice  ──┬── Slack Bot
                       │
                       └── Web Dashboard
```
X

Example 1: Podcast Guest Research Microservice

- **Input:** Guest name + podcast they appeared on
- **Process:** Execute search → Analyze transcript → Generate brief
- **Output:** 1-2-page media brief with background, key points, and notable quotes

Multiple Interface Deployment:

- Marketing team accesses via CRM button labeled "Generate Media Brief"
- Host prep team uses Slack command `/guestbrief John Smith on AI Today`
- Content team embeds in their editorial dashboard

Example 2: Meeting Scheduling Assistant Microservice

- **Input:** Request details (attendees, desired time frame, meeting purpose)
- **Process:** Analyze calendars → Generate proposed times › Execute calendar invites upon confirmation
- **Output:** Scheduled meeting invite sent to all attendees

The 8 Core LLM Tasks

These fundamental capabilities are the building blocks for microservices. A typical microservice combines 1-3 of these tasks.

Task	What It Does (Enhanced Description)	Example Application
Execute	Triggers external actions or API calls (*e.g., run search, use tool*)	"Search online for [person]'s recent podcast appearances"
Extract	Pulls specific, *often structured*, data points from given content	"Get all mentions of 'AI strategy' from the provided transcript"
Summarize	Condenses longer content, *preserving core meaning & key info*	"Create a 3-point summary of this hour-long episode transcript"
Analyze	*Understands content*, identifies patterns, interprets meaning, insights	"Based on these interview transcripts, what themes appeared most often?"
Generate	Creates *new/original* content by *synthesizing provided inputs*	"Using the analyzed insights above, draft a personalized outreach email."
Transform	Converts content to a new format, style, or structure; *preserves meaning*	"Convert this technical explanation paragraph into bullet points for executives"

Edit	Improves existing content *for quality, clarity, grammar, or tone*	"Make this draft email more persuasive while maintaining a formal tone"
Classify	Categorizes input text into *predefined* labels or classes	"Is this customer email response 'Positive', 'Negative', or 'Neutral'?"

Implementation Guidelines:

- Each microservice should perform a single, well-defined task identified in your Stage 1 role template.

- A task typically involves chaining 1-3 of the core LLM functions. More complex operations should be broken down into multiple collaborating microservices (leading towards Stage 3).

- Design each microservice with a clear API endpoint for clean integration.

- Build for interface-agnostic deployment to maximize utility across teams and platforms.

- Starting with these focused services allows you to **test AI ROI** on a limited scale, **minimize disruption**, and **lay the foundation** for more complex agentic workflows later.

Transition to Stage 3 & 4:

At Stage 2, these tools still generally require human direction or orchestration. In Stages 3 (Agentic Workflows) and 4 (Drop-in AI Coworkers), intelligence layers coordinate multiple agentic tools and microservices into autonomous systems, significantly reducing or eliminating the need for direct human management of the process flow.

Stage 3: Agentic Workflows (Complete)

Connected tools with human guidance for process efficiency

Stage 3 combines multiple Stage 2 microservices into coordinated workflows, requiring strategic human involvement only at key decision points.

Key Characteristics:

- **Workflow Orchestration:** Coordinates a sequence of Stage 2 microservices
- **Strategic Human Touchpoints:** Human judgment only for crucial decisions
- **Process Awareness:** Understands the entire workflow and maintains state
- **Tactical Autonomy:** Handles execution steps independently
- **Smart Routing:** Directs workflow based on intermediate outcomes

Architectural Transition:

```
Xgraph TD
    A[Human Strategy Direction] --> B[Workflow
Coordination Layer]
    B --> C1[Microservice 1: Research]
    C1 --> B
    B --> C2[Microservice 2: Content Creation]
    C2 --> B
    B --> D[Human Checkpoint: Strategic Choices]
    D --> B
    B --> C3[Microservice 3: Logistics]
```

```
C3 --> B
style A fill:#d0e0ff,stroke:#0077cc
style B fill:#ffe6cc,stroke:#cc7000
style C1 fill:#d5f5d5,stroke:#2d882d
style C2 fill:#d5f5d5,stroke:#2d882d
style C3 fill:#d5f5d5,stroke:#2d882d
style D fill:#f9d5e5,stroke:#d64161
```
✕

Notice how human checkpoints are minimized to only the most critical decision points.

Example: Podcast Outreach Workflow

A realistic Stage 3 podcast outreach workflow:

1. AI research tool generates a list of potential podcasts based on client criteria

2. **Human selects the most appropriate shows** from the AI-curated list (strategic taste)

3. Personalization engine creates and sends custom pitches for selected shows (no review needed)

4. Response analyzer classifies incoming replies (positive, negative, needs clarification)

5. For positive responses, **human handles the actual booking** (relationship management)

6. System tracks all communication and maintains the outreach pipeline

This workflow eliminates routine tasks while preserving human expertise for strategic selection and relationship-building during the booking phase.

The KOODAR Framework: Documenting Roles for AI Workflows

To build effective Stage 3 systems, we need a comprehensive framework for defining exactly what the workflow needs to understand and how it should operate. The KOODAR framework provides this structure:

```
✕K - KNOW: Information sources and mission foundation
O - OBSERVE: Assessment of current state
O - ORIENT: Establishing context and baselines
D - DECIDE: Framework for choices and boundaries
A - ACT: Standard procedures and exception handling
R - REVIEW: Evaluation and communication
✕
```

Stage 3 Implementation Focus: KD-AR

While the complete KOODAR framework defines a full AI coworker role (Stage 4), Stage 3 workflows typically implement only four of these six capabilities:

K - KNOW (Information Sources)

- What information the workflow needs access to
- Which knowledge bases and documentation to integrate
- What data restrictions apply to this process

D - DECIDE (Decision Boundaries)

- Clear criteria for which decisions can be automated vs. require human input
- What escalation thresholds trigger human intervention
- What compliance requirements must be maintained

A - ACT (Standard Procedures)

- Documented workflow steps for routine scenarios
- How to interact with existing systems and teams

R - REVIEW (Evaluation)

- Performance tracking and reporting
- Success metrics and feedback mechanisms

The middle capabilities (OBSERVE and ORIENT) typically require more sophisticated context understanding and are usually reserved for Stage 4 implementation.

Practical Application: Podcast Outreach KOODAR Template

Let's see how KOODAR documents our podcast outreach workflow example:

K - KNOW (Information Sources)

Information streams:

- Client brand guidelines and messaging
- Database of podcast hosts and contact information
- CRM records of past interactions with hosts
- Performance metrics on historical pitches

Success metrics:

- Booking rate: Successful placements / total outreach attempts
- Response rate: Replies received / emails sent
- Completion time: Days from initial outreach to confirmed booking

D - DECIDE (Decision Boundaries)

Automated decisions:

- Initial research list generation
- Personalization of approved templates
- Classification of standard responses
- Follow-up scheduling and reminders

Human decisions required:

- Final podcast selection from researched options
- Negotiation of non-standard appearance terms
- Resolution of complex scheduling conflicts
- Handling sensitive reputation management issues

Escalation triggers:

- Host requests unusual accommodations
- Negative sentiment detected in host responses
- Potential brand misalignment identified
- Scheduling conflicts without clear resolution

A - ACT (Standard Procedures)

Research procedure:

- Generate initial list of 20+ potential podcasts
- Apply relevance scoring based on topic alignment
- Check for audience size and engagement metrics
- Verify recent activity (published in last 60 days)
- Present options with scoring rationale to human

Outreach procedure:

- Generate personalized pitches from approved templates

- Send initial contact on optimal day/time
- Track opens and responses in CRM
- Classify responses and route accordingly
- Generate appropriate follow-ups for non-responses
- Route positive responses to human for relationship management

R - REVIEW (Evaluation)

Performance tracking:

- Weekly dashboard showing outreach volume, response rate, booking rate
- Comparison of performance across different pitch templates
- Analysis of which podcast categories yield highest success rates
- Tag successful approaches for template improvement
- Document host preferences for future interactions
- Update personalization algorithms based on response data

This KOODAR documentation provides a comprehensive blueprint for building the workflow, clearly delineating what the system needs to handle versus where human judgment is required.

Implementation Approach: Building Stage 3 Workflows

Converting your KOODAR documentation into functioning Stage 3 systems involves:

1. Define Integration Architecture

- Select an orchestration platform (Airflow, Prefect, or custom)
- Map data flows between microservices
- Establish API contracts for each service

2. Implement Human Touchpoints

- Design intuitive dashboards for decision points
- Create clear notification systems for escalations
- Enable contextual information display at decision moments

3. Build Monitoring and Analytics

- Track process volume, velocity, and outcomes
- Identify bottlenecks and failure points
- Measure ROI against manual process baselines

4. Start with Minimal Viable Workflow

- Begin with core capabilities and limited scope
- Maintain parallel manual processes during testing
- Gradually expand automation scope as confidence builds

Stage 3 Limitations and Path to Stage 4

Stage 3 workflows still operate within clearly defined parameters and lack the full autonomy of Stage 4 AI coworkers. Key limitations include:

- **Limited Context Understanding:** They follow predefined paths rather than truly "understanding" the business context

- **Reactive Rather Than Proactive:** They respond to triggers and timers rather than independently identifying opportunities

- **Rigid Decision Boundaries:** They have difficulty applying judgment to novel situations

- **Process-Centric, Not Role-Centric:** They handle workflows rather than adapting to take ownership of outcomes

These limitations define the boundary between Stage 3 and Stage 4 implementations.

Stage 4: Drop-in AI Coworkers

Full role replacement for consistent, scalable teams Stage 4 represents the pinnacle of AI implementation. Autonomous systems that function as complete team members, taking ownership of entire responsibility areas with minimal supervision.

NOT AGI

When we refer to a "Drop In Coworker" we actually mean a specialized freelancer or productized service equivalent. A discrete scalable ruleset for the role, but not a learning and growing being who can take on any task.

At this point (early 2025) it is not possible to run reliable generalized agents in production/enterprise settings.

Key Characteristics:

- **Full KOODAR Implementation:** All six capabilities, including advanced contextual understanding
- **Human-Like Collaboration:** Natural communication and adaptation to team norms
- **Proactive Task Identification:** Independently recognizes needs and opportunities
- **Responsibility Ownership:** Accountable for outcomes, not just processes
- **Judgment Application:** Makes complex decisions within defined parameters

Architectural Evolution:

```
Xgraph TD
    A[Human Manager] -.strategic direction.-> B[AI
Coworker]
    B -->|Manages| C1[Workflow 1]
    B -->|Manages| C2[Workflow 2]
    B -->|Manages| C3[Workflow 3]
    B -->|Requests help| A
    C1 -.-> B
    C2 -.-> B
    C3 -.-> B
    style A fill:#d0e0ff,stroke:#0077cc
    style B fill:#f9d5e5,stroke:#d64161
    style C1 fill:#ffe6cc,stroke:#cc7000
    style C2 fill:#ffe6cc,stroke:#cc7000
    style C3 fill:#ffe6cc,stroke:#cc7000
X
```

The critical shift: AI coworkers now manage entire workflows and only consult humans for strategic guidance, reversing the relationship seen in Stage 3.

Complete KOODAR Implementation

Stage 4 fully implements all six KOODAR capabilities, with particular emphasis on the previously limited OBSERVE and ORIENT functions:

O - OBSERVE (Assessment of Current State)

- Monitors performance against established goals
- Identifies patterns and anomalies requiring attention
- Recognizes key indicators signaling need for action

O - ORIENT (Establishing Context)

- Maintains awareness of baseline performance

- Aligns activities with broader organizational goals
- Performs comparative analysis to guide decisions

These capabilities enable AI coworkers to function with significantly greater autonomy, adapting to changing conditions rather than simply following predefined workflows.

Example: Podcast Booking AI Coworker

A Stage 4 podcast booking AI coworker named "BookingAI":

1. **Manages the entire booking function** with minimal supervision

2. **Proactively researches** new podcasts aligned with client positioning

3. **Develops and tests** different outreach strategies

4. **Analyzes performance patterns** and adapts approaches accordingly

5. **Identifies strategic opportunities** like trending topics or competitive gaps

6. **Makes judgment calls** on which hosts to prioritize based on complex factors

7. **Handles routine relationship management,** escalating only unusual situations

8. **Provides strategic recommendations** on client messaging and target shows

The human manager shifts from day-to-day direction to periodic reviews and strategic guidance.

Prime Candidates for Stage 4 Implementation

Initial Stage 4 deployments typically succeed in roles with:

- **Well-defined boundaries:** Clear scope and measurable outcomes

- **Structured interactions:** Predictable communication patterns

- **Digital-native workflows:** Primarily online processes and tools

- **Moderate judgment requirements:** Complex but bounded decision spaces

Specific examples include:

1. Customer Support Representatives

- Handle tier-1 support queries with consistent quality
- Manage appropriate escalation to specialists
- Maintain comprehensive interaction documentation

2. SDRs

- Research leads
- Write outreach messages
- Follow up and route to AE on response

3. Content Production Specialists

- Create consistent, on-brand content from templates
- Adapt messaging for different channels
- Maintain publishing schedules

Implementation Framework: Full KOODAR Documentation

Implementing a Stage 4 AI coworker requires complete documentation of all six KOODAR elements. Here's an abbreviated example for a Podcast Booking AI Coworker:

K - KNOW

- Comprehensive access to client positioning, industry trends, podcast landscape
- Integration with email, calendar, CRM, and media monitoring systems
- Clear metrics: booking volume, quality tier placements, client satisfaction

O - OBSERVE

- Continuous monitoring of outreach response rates across different approaches
- Analysis of timing patterns (day/week/month) affecting success rates
- Identification of emerging podcast formats or platforms
- Detection of shifts in host preferences or booking processes

O - ORIENT

- Regular benchmarking against historical performance
- Comparison of results across different client industries
- Alignment of booking targets with client business objectives
- Understanding current PR landscape and media consumption trends

D - DECIDE

- Clear prioritization framework for podcast selection
- Ethical and compliance guidelines for outreach
- Defined thresholds for when to escalate unusual requests
- Boundaries of authority for scheduling and content approvals

A - ACT

- Comprehensive procedures for research, outreach, booking, and follow-up
- Exception handling protocols for non-standard situations
- Communication templates and personalization guidelines

R - REVIEW

- Regular performance reporting to stakeholders
- Systems for incorporating feedback into future approaches
- Documentation of successful strategies for knowledge base
- Mechanisms for continuous improvement of processes

ABOUT DIGITAL OPERATIONS INSITITUTE

Digital Operations Institute (DOI) is the premiere educator, trainer, and publisher of books on digital operations, AI, automation, and business transformation.

About 3rd brain Digital Operations

Most SMBs are racing into AI without the operational foundation to support it - leading to security risks, tech debt, and wasted spending on tools their teams won't adopt.

We assess your digital operations maturity, build a strategic roadmap, then provide the training, fractional expertise and long-term talent you need to execute it.

You're not just advised what to do but are actively building the internal capacity to maintain and grow your digital operations flywheel.

3rd Brain Digital Operations is one of the founding members of DOI. Learn more at 3rdbrain.co

www.ingramcontent.com/pod-product-compliance
Lightning Source LLC
Chambersburg PA
CBHW031959190326
41520CB00007B/297